UNLOCKED

Essential Keys to Manage Family Conflict

ANGELA MITAKIDIS
SHANNON R. BROWN

With Foreword by Dr. John Ng

Edited by Lisa Best

Publishing Director: Dr. Michael Mitakidis

Print ISBN: 978-1-66782-809-1
eBook ISBN: 978-1-66782-810-7

We dedicate this book to our family, friends, mentors, and most importantly, to our Lord. Through Him, all things, especially reconciliation, are possible.

Conflict and resolution are two sides of the same coin.

—Haresh Sippy

Contents

Foreword

What I hear, I forget

What I see, I remember

What I do becomes a part of me

—Confucius

Although I am a student and researcher in conflict management, I am a conflict management practitioner at heart. Unlocked is a book that I not only enjoyed reading but has equipped me with many practical conflict management frameworks and tips. The authors' easy-reading, informal style makes the ideas and concepts so palatable.

Both Angela and Shannon are practitioners, not just theoreticians who are stuck in the ivory tower of academia. They have made references to many well-documented studies and thought-leaders in this field to substantiate their approach. They desire to help individuals and families confront conflicts, manage them, recover from them and equip us with practical skills to manage conflict more effectively.

What I enjoyed about Angela and Shannon is their authenticity, humility and practicality.

Authenticity

They openly share their struggles and issues in conflict management. They enriched me with their many personal anecdotes and examples, which are so rich and real. Their stories resonated with me and made me feel they understand my struggles in conflict. They have provided me with tips that I can use immediately. Most of all, they give me hope even when I have messed up in my conflicts. I can recover. I can be forgiven and learn to forgive.

Humility

Another aspect that stands out for me in this book is the humility of Angela and Shannon. They are willing to expose their vulnerabilities and candidly discuss their weaknesses. This revealed their transparent posture and made them so relatable. They do not stand from a high horse, pontificating, but shoulder-to-shoulder with me. And at times on bended knees to encourage me in this difficult journey of family conflicts.

Practicality

They provide many useful frameworks I appreciated and benefited from. *They are briefly mentioned below.*

In Part I, The 7 Stages in the family life cycle provides a good framework to help me understand my family development and its complexities.

In Part II, the Amygdala Hijack explains why emotions like fear and anger are difficult to manage. The chapter on adolescence is one of the best chapters, helping me appreciate the teenage brain. Using Daniel Siegel's framework, they unpacked the upside and downside of the teenage brain. Besides debunking certain stereotypes about teens, they laid out facts in a most cogent and practical manner. One of the most valuable tips is their assertion that parents who shift from a teaching role to a mentoring role during adolescence may be more successful by fostering a positive relationship with their teens. Such parents will also forge a better relationship with them into their adult years.

Beyond laying out the terrains of family and the genesis of family conflict, their most hands-on chapters are laid out in Part III of the book, The Toolkit, which most appropriately, they expend the most time on. This part is their unique contribution to the field of conflict management.

In the chapter on Naming the Pain, their clever use of the acronym NAME makes it helpful in the recall. The PEACE Toolkit which they so clearly elucidated is another example of a conceptual framework, which connects and resonates with me. Acknowledging our propensity for anger, their relational saver's HAT perspective also provides a very important skill set. It is truly a 'Homicide Avoidance Toolkit'. Their various tips, with interesting imagery names, like The Oxygen Pump, The Exit Sign, The Elliptical, The Wilson, The Leaf Blower, The Stud Finder, The Heart Monitor, The Freezer and The Stationery are so concrete and useful.

Finally, their last two sections on family forgiveness and family are so needed today, especially in these challenging times of COVID and the new normal. They made me reflect on how I can keep my family whole.

Angela and Shannon, thank you for making such an important contribution to this area of conflict management. I believe a book is only good if I put into practice what I learned. That's why I started my foreword with the Chinese Proverb by Confucius:

> What I hear, I forget
> What I see, I remember
> What I do becomes a part of me

So, make effective conflict management a part of your life by practicing these principles!

John Ng, Ph.D.
Chief Passionary Officer
Meta Consulting
Author of the best-selling book *Smiling Tiger, Hidden Dragon: Managing Conflict @ Work and Home*

Preface

As a mediator and teacher, I teach individuals to manage, resolve and mediate all kinds of conflicts. Many of these are family conflict cases including divorce, custody and child support. Whether or not a conflict directly involves a family, one thing is clear: Our families of origin have impacted how we understand conflict, how we react to conflict and ultimately how we manage conflict.

This book is about opening our understanding of the nature and anatomy of family dynamics. This is not only an invaluable exercise in understanding how we manage conflicts within our own families, but a step toward recognizing that others have their own way of handling conflicts too —not always wrong—just different from ours.

Such an understanding will go a long way in equipping oneself in the effective use of tools and techniques of conflict resolution. These tools and techniques can be learned by anyone willing to live a more peaceful life. This book is a consolidation of many years in the legal and dispute resolution field, as well as my own life experiences.

Whether you are a student using this book as a resource or someone who has faced a fair amount of conflict in life, this book will be a valuable guide because we all began life's journey in a family.

Angela Mitakidis

This book began when my co-author was discussing a need for one single textbook for her class on the dynamics of family conflict. In her search for reading materials for her course, she had to acquire a number of resources to cover both academic and practical application material on the specific topics she desired to impart to her students.

Our collaboration came out of a dear friendship when she asked me a simple question: "How do you handle being angry with someone you must stay in a relationship with?" At the time she posed the question, neither of us knew that it would lead to this partnership—a partnership that resulted in fulfilling a need neither of us realized existed. Our hope is to use our combined knowledge and experience to help families in conflict—and those that serve and minister to them—weather storms and come out stronger on the other side.

Shannon R. Brown

Acknowledgements

While there are many, many people involved in the production of this book, there are a few we would like to thank individually.

It is with deepest gratitude that we thank Dr. John Ng for his wisdom, encouragement and agreeing to write the foreword for our book. Thank you for blazing the trail in this peacemaking business we all inhabit. You have improved the lives of so many through your work, including ours. We know, without a doubt, that without your work, ours would not exist.

We would also like to thank the many colleagues and professionals that agreed to read our book providing valuable feedback and, in some cases, the endorsements you will find on the back cover of our book. Thanks for this assistance goes to Professor Joey Cope, Mun Loon Lai, Loong Seng Onn, Judge Andrea Plumlee, Dr. John Potter and Dr. Dewey Wilson. Your encouragement and support have been invaluable.

Thanks also goes to our beta readers—the entirety of the SMU Fall 2018 Family Conflict class with special thanks to Supritha Arsikere, Lara Bailey, Stan Heston, Chante Little, Cailtin Robb and Elizabeth Cuevan Thompson. Your feedback throughout the semester and your detailed notes on the book survey was invaluable in helping us improve and expand upon our material. As the first readers of our full manuscript you will always have a special place in our hearts.

Additionally, we would like to thank Jessica Lunce. Thank you for all of your support, encouragement and early editing help. You have been with this project from its inception and a valuable sounding board.

Finally, to our editor Lisa Best. Your tireless efforts to refine and improve this book were invaluable. Thank you for your expertise, insightful questions and helping us get this project across the finish line.

Angela and Shannon

To my sidekick, best friend, and love of my life, Mike. Thank you doesn't begin to express my gratitude for being with me every step of the way on this life journey we embarked on together 30 years ago. You and I, what a ride, what an adventure. Thank you for the love and laughter you continue to pour into our marriage and family. To my darlings, Keziah and Matthew, you have been so gracious to me as we have navigated this parenting thing! You are my pride and joy and I love you fiercely. To my co-author and friend, Shannon, thank you for the endless hours of writing and championing our work to its final completion. Finally, to my Lord and Savior, who gave me the passion, drive, and opportunities to pursue my dreams.

Angela

I absolutely could not have collaborated on this book without the support and assistance of my family and my friends. There are not enough words to express my gratitude to those that have come alongside me during my lifetime. Some have been here for a season, others a lifetime. My husband, Aaron, and children, Sierra and Tanner, have supported me from the beginning, encouraging—and at times cajoling—me to pursue my lifelong desire to put pen to paper. My friend and co-author, Angela recognized a desire in myself before I even did and asked me to join her in this endeavor. Finally, I must give a shout out to the Lord. He knew exactly what pieces needed to come together and the perfect timing for it all.

Shannon

Introduction

> Techniques are like tools: The more you have, the more options for getting a job done but you have to know what you are building first.
>
> —Joseph A. Micucci, *The Adolescent in Family Therapy: Harnessing the Power of Relationship*

Family. The very word means different things to different people. For some it is a reminder of a warm and nurturing environment they long to return to; for others it is a reminder of a tumultuous and contentious environment they ran from as soon as possible. Others long for the family they feel they never had. The reaction to the word *family* is as complex as each individual that exists. While there is great variety in one's reaction to the word, one thing is for certain: Family is difficult to define and often elicits strong emotions.

There is no denying the importance of the family unit when it comes to the functioning of society at large. Without families, there would be no future generations; they provide the basic survival and educational needs for each new generation. The more well-functioning families in the world, the better the health of society in general.

While the composition, definition and emotional reactions the word family elicits vary widely, there is something that all families experience at one time or another: conflict. A person's first experience with conflict usually occurs at home during childhood. It may be a disagreement with a sibling over a toy, a scolding from a parent or even witnessing a conflict between parents. Conflict arises within families and affects every member of that family at one time or another.

Similarly, how conflict is managed in the family of origin impacts the way an individual learns to deal with conflict. If a family faces conflict head-on, determined to resolve it, that often becomes the approach a child will take with them as they leave home. If conflict is avoided at all costs, it is common for the children from such a family to shy away from conflict later in life. This is underscored when one understands that behavior modeling is one of the most effective modes of instruction.

Addressing and reconciling conflict within families is challenging as there is no single solution for every situation. Those seeking to assist families in crisis, be it friends, clinicians, mediators, etc., must have a wide and varied selection of skills and tools at their disposal. The following chapters contain a treasure trove of these tips and tools presented as keys. As we discuss these keys, we will on occasion discuss a specific clinician, researcher or author who has influenced our work. However, the foundation for these keys is our personal and professional experiences.

Moving through the text, we encourage readers to pick up each key and put it on their own conflict management key ring. Some readers may find that a version of some of these keys already hangs from their ring, while others may find a completely new set of keys. Whether you envisage using any number of the keys contained in this text or not, we encourage you to add them to your key ring. Someday you may need one of those keys you were tempted to leave sitting on the table at home—it may open a valuable door of healing, reconciliation, forgiveness, resilience and much more for yourself, your family or another family in crisis.

Our hope and prayer is that this book will not only educate and equip the reader to handle conflict more effectively, but it will also emphasize that conflict is not necessarily negative. When conflict is viewed as an opportunity to grow, learn, heal and get to know one another more intimately, it can free a family from the destruction that conflict can potentially bring. Conflict is normal. As long as we have breath, we will have conflict. Let's learn to do this better.

The information shared in this book is meant for informational and educational purposes only. It is not designed to take the place of a licensed counselor, medical professional, lawyer, etc. This resource touches on some very sensitive topics that may make you aware of issues in your own life that you were not yet conscious of. If you find yourself having difficulty with any issues that arise as a result of your self-reflection, it is imperative that you seek out the appropriate professional resource.

Part I:
Anatomy of a Family

Chapter 1
Defining Family

No one fights dirtier or more brutally than blood; only family knows its own weaknesses, the exact placement of the heart. The tragedy is that one can still live with the force of hatred, feel infuriated that once you are born to another, that kinship lasts through life and death, immutable, unchanging, no matter how great the misdeed or betrayal. Blood cannot be denied, and perhaps that's why we fight tooth and claw, because we cannot—being only human—put asunder what God has joined together.

—Whitney Otto, *How to Make an American Quilt*

The family is the first essential cell of human society.

—Pope John XXIII

What Is a Family?

Before one begins to explore the nature of family conflict, the question that must be answered is how one defines a family. This may sound like something we should already be familiar with and clear about. However, on closer examination we come to realize that the definition of *family* is as unique and diverse as each family unit and the individuals within those units.

In defining *family*, apart from one's own personal view of what constitutes a family, we encounter religious, social and legal definitions. Historically, in the United States, the trend has been to define a "traditional" family as a nuclear family, that is, a family made up of father, mother and children. This definition of family is no longer broad enough, especially considering the legal changes in the 21st century.

The last hundred years have seen more change in nearly all areas of life than any other preceding century. Information technology -and with it, social media—has taken the world by storm. Globalization is no longer a futuristic possibility, it's a present reality. Artificial intelligence is not only vastly utilized but is being refined as we speak. Biotechnology has rapidly developed. The definition of marriage has been legally altered. The architecture of family structures in society today is exponentially more diverse than ever before. What defines a family must therefore be examined and explored so that we are able to dialogue from a common understanding. This does not imply that we will necessarily agree with all the changes we see, but whether we agree (or even like it) or not, we are living in this new world. Social media has ensured that no one is unaware of social diversity today. As we attempt to help families maneuver through conflict, we have to acknowledge these changes and decide whether we will be an instrument of peaceful navigation in this time of rapid world change, or a contributor to further division.

Definitions of Family

The Merriam Webster dictionary offers a variety of definitions for the word *family*. One broad definition is a group of individuals living under one roof, usually under one head, that is, a household. Another says a group of persons under common ancestry.[1] A nuclear family is considered a family group that consists only of parents and children.[2] The "traditional" family is defined as "the basic unit in society traditionally consisting of two parents rearing their children."[3]

Defining what constitutes a family is not as straightforward as it may seem. It is also heavily influenced by the culture in which a family unit lives, and it continues to evolve over time. At the dawn of the 20th century in the United States (US), a family was typically defined as being nuclear in nature: two parents and their children.[4]

This traditional definition appears to be the model upon which the US Census Bureau defines family:[5]

- **Family**: a group of two people or more, related to each other by birth, marriage or adoption, residing together and considered as members of one family.
- **Family Household**: maintained by a householder who is in a family, and includes unrelated people who may be residing there. Family members, however, are people related to one another as per the definition of family above.

While these may be the most efficient definitions for census taking, they fail to account for the vast diversity of current family makeup. The US has often been referred to as a "nation of immigrants." As people have emigrated to the US from all over the world, they have brought aspects of their culture with them, including their definition of family. Whether they came on the Mayflower, or through Ellis Island, as slaves or refugees, immigrants' culture of origin inform their—and consequently our—definition of *family*. These cultures vary greatly from one end of the spectrum, viewing one's family unit as those living in the house, to the other, which includes ancestors in the definition of a family unit. The fabric of American society is therefore interwoven with these views.

Ancestors

I recall our early days in Singapore when we were confused by small heaps of oranges, cakes and burning incense placed on the front porches of houses or at the basement of apartment buildings. On enquiring about these types of rituals from locals, we were informed that these acts are a form of respect and honor to the memories of ancestors. Family is viewed as a unit of living relatives as well as ancestors. The belief is that deceased family members continue to live and that their spirits continue to take an active role in the living family and its well-being. Ancestors are therefore venerated by making offerings to them. The food offered is in honor of the nourishment provided by ancestors when family members were growing up. Similarly, in my country of origin (South Africa) ancestors remain an integral part of a family's spirituality.

—Angela Mitakidis

The Family of Choice

The idea of extending a family beyond blood ties is not new; however, in recent years it has become more widely accepted. This concept of a "family of choice" has been embraced in recent generations. A chosen family may include blood or adoptive relations, but there is no requirement for a chosen family to have biological and/or legal ties.

In these types of families, the emotional bond of its members is the most important defining factor. In the 1960s and early 1970s, communes were a good example of a chosen family. Each member of a commune had a responsibility to contribute to the community, just as each member of a family is expected to contribute to the family.

With the rise of dual-income and single-parent homes there has been an increase in the need to go beyond one's blood relatives to help care for children, homes, and so forth.[6] This concept has become so accepted in our current society that the dictionary includes this idea as one of its definitions of family: "a group of people united by certain convictions or a common affiliation."[7] We encourage you to take time to ponder other types of families you are aware of in your own circle and community that may be defined as a family of choice.

My Chosen Family

My friend Laura is a medical professional with two children a few years younger than my kids. When her youngest was one, she suddenly found herself divorced with custody of the kids and little financial support from her ex-husband. It was imperative that she continue to work to provide for herself and her children. Additionally, her ex-husband was a stay-at-home parent which left her in need of childcare. Thankfully, Laura had a family that could help her with some of the childcare, but needed someone else to cover the rest of the time. This is where I came in. I was already at home with my kids so I offered to fill in the gaps.

When the arrangement started, our kids were merely acquaintances. They had gotten along in the past, but hadn't really spent a lot of time together. This dynamic slowly began to change as the years went by and our families began to spend more and more time together, including on holidays. My relationship with Laura developed into more of a sisterhood than mere friendship. As our friendship deepened, so did the relationships between our kids. At first, they went from acquaintances to friends, then became more like cousins, and finally came to the place where they consider themselves siblings. The kids became so used to relating as siblings that I had to answer some interesting questions from curious outsiders when one of the kids included their non-blood-related sibling on their family tree. Myself, Laura, my husband and our kids created our own family: a family of choice.

This is just one example of a family of choice. I assure you that we had family conflict at times. Thankfully, having developed good conflict management skills we have always been able to resolve our differences.

—Shannon Brown

Working with the Family's Definition

Through our own experiences it has become clear that it is often critical for those of us working with families to set aside our own notion of what a family is. Instead, we need to understand the definition embraced by the family we are dealing with, in other words, how they define themselves. Additionally, it is important to acknowledge their definition and then work within their definitive framework. Expressing acceptance of each family's own definition positions you as an ally of the family. Becoming an ally often goes a long way in gaining the trust and cooperation of that family, and ultimately increases the efficacy of the work you propose to do within that family.

Be it a single-parent family, a family with two mothers or two fathers, one that includes stepparents and siblings, a two-parent heterosexual family, a grandparent-led family, a multi-generational family or a chosen family, we believe that the ultimate goal is to encourage sufficient unity and resilience for optimal family functioning. The family of choice is a way to reconcile a general definition of a family, one that is particularly useful when assistance with family conflict management is requested.

It is important to note that when dealing with family conflict, it is imperative to be mindful of the parameters of your current legal system.

The circumstances in which a person is assisting a family in conflict is key in determining the appropriate definition of family. If it is in a legal matter, then the legal definition of family must supersede any other definition. In a nonlegal situation, it may be advantageous to have a more fluid definition of family. The goal in either situation is to ensure that the conflict is alleviated in a manner that is as positive an outcome as possible for each member, regardless of how the family defines itself.

When working to mitigate conflict within families, it is imperative that we are cognizant of each family's own unique design, structure and self-definition.

Chapter 2
Family Psychology: A Bird's Eye View

Be who you are and say what you feel because those who
mind don't matter and those who matter don't mind.

—Dr. Seuss

Behavioral Blueprint

While conflict and dysfunction have been a part of family life since
its inception, the idea that a family can be improved with external help and
counsel is a relatively new idea. It was a natural extension of the formal-
ization of the study of both psychology and sociology.

Dr. Sigmund Freud founded the practice of psychoanalysis in the
late 19th and early 20th centuries. Freud believed that spending time with
patients discussing their life experiences, including their formative years
in their childhood homes, allows for an individual to identify areas of
difficulty in their life and improve their own behavior.[1]

In the 1940s, Dr. Carl Rogers developed a new therapeutic model
that was coined "self-actualization." In this model, the clinician relies
on the belief that humans have an innate desire to improve their life and
circumstances. As such, a clinician should be focused on guiding clients
to discover their own areas of weakness and how they might address them.
Rogers employed the use of probing questions allowing clients to come to
their own conclusions about their interpersonal difficulties.[2]

While they may have differed on their method of treatment, both
Freud and Rogers contributed to early family counseling. In the 1940s

and 1950s, counseling focused on individuals. The idea was that improved individual behavior would lead to improved family function. It viewed a family as separate with distinct parts that should be addressed as such. The idea that the family is an actual unit, and should be treated as its own entity, developed later.

Dr. Alfred Adler, a contemporary of Freud, was the first clinician to perform family therapy. Adler believed that early childhood was incredibly influential in a person's development. As such, he began to focus on the family as a unit. This idea influenced the expansion of his therapeutic model to include other members of the family. Adler posited that not only is individual change necessary for assisting dysfunctional families, but the family as a whole need to make adjustments as well. Adler's ideas laid the groundwork for our current family therapy models.[3]

Today, therapeutic models tend to focus on the dynamics of the family unit and how they impact the well-being of the individual. In individual therapy, clinicians often spend time discussing their client's family of origin to assist in the identification of underlying issues that contribute to that person's mental health, or lack thereof. Using this information, the client and clinician construct a blueprint for problematic behavior and habits. Once this blueprint has been laid out, it allows for an understanding of why certain dysfunction plagues an individual, and gives clues as to what needs to be learned and/or unlearned. By identifying harmful behaviors learned in the family of origin, the individual is able to learn new behaviors, thereby leading to a healthier and more satisfying life.

In family therapy, the behavioral blueprint allows for the family and clinician to identify areas of concern and then decipher healthier behavioral alternatives. While it may require changes on the part of individual family members, the focus in family therapy is to improve the function of the family as a whole.

Family Systems Theory

Dr. Murray Bowen was the first to begin to approach the family unit as an organism unto itself. He believed it was important to study not just the individuals in a family, but also their interactions and how they function as a unit. In the 1950s he spent time observing several families with a schizophrenic member. At first, he was only interested in the mother-child interactions, but then expanded his focus to include all members of the family of origin. What he learned in those observations led him to develop his Family Systems Theory (FST).[4]

FST views family as an emotional unit best understood when analyzed within a multigenerational or historical framework. In other words, time must be spent identifying how the family interacts—and even how the families of origin of the parental figures in a family interacted —to get a clear picture of how to assist a dysfunctional family. Bowen believed that the driving force of all human behavior derives from the ebb and flow of family life. This transgenerational focus helps to identify current problematic behaviors that may be caused by unresolved issues within the family of origin. Once those issues have been identified, it is easier to determine how best to change the current functioning of the family unit.[5]

FST is steeped in evolutionary theory. It theorizes the reason families are connected on an emotional level is because that type of bond is required to provide for the basic needs of the family: food, shelter and protection. This necessary interdependence for survival led to an emotional interdependence as well. Bowen took this evolutionary approach beyond just the basic needs for survival. His theory also considers human emotional functioning to be subject to the same set of laws that govern other systems in nature. Each individual member of the family, their role, their stage in life, etc. has an impact on the function of the whole unit. Therefore, any attempt to assist a family in crisis must be cognizant of both the physical and emotional needs of the family; this is considered crucial to the success of a family.[6]

FST explores how family members often begin to absorb and mimic the feelings of their siblings/parents. For example, if there is financial stress that has the parents wondering if they will be able to keep a roof over the family's heads, the children will often feel that stress and take it on as their own, even if they are unaware of the financial issues.[7]

When contending with an emotional crisis, each individual must be aware of their role in the situation and then be willing to acknowledge and deal with not only their feelings, but also those of other family members. The interdependence of family members often gives rise to an internal conflict: the push and pull between self-focus and other-focus. This is a hallmark of the human condition and it impacts the functioning of a family or marriage. This struggle with the interdependence of family members often leaves people in a battle with themselves and each other.

As humans, particularly in the US, there is a deeply held belief that we need individual autonomy—the need to put ourselves first and be self-sufficient. At the same time, there is the human need for companionship and relationship with other humans. Typically, these first battles between self and others happen in our family of origin. One of the difficulties of maintaining an emotionally satisfying familial relationship is to find a balance between the need for togetherness and each member's need for autonomy. The ability to strike that balance often determines the health of the family unit and even the health of the next generation's familial relationships. After all, beyond the basic needs of food, water and shelter, the quality of our relationships most often determines the quality of our lives.

Choice Theory and Reality Therapy

The preceding discussion brings us aptly into an examination of the late Dr. William Glasser's work, which has had a profound influence on our own lives and our work. As a psychiatrist, Glasser focuses on the choices that individuals make and how they affect their relationships and own emotional functionality. Using the concept of individual choice as his cornerstone, Glasser devised a behavioral theory known as *choice theory*.

The basic tenets of choice theory posit that every human being has five basic needs: survival, love and belonging, power, freedom and fun. These are defined as follows:[8]

- Survival: The need to be fed, sheltered and clothed. This also includes the experience of sexual satisfaction.
- Love and belonging: The need for relationship with others, be that in a family, social or work setting.
- Power: The need to find self-worth through the ability to win and dominate.
- Freedom: The need to feel in control of one's own destiny and not beholden to others.
- Fun: The need to feel content and satisfied, and the ability to enjoy life and activities.

Glasser's 1999 identification of these basic needs led him to develop a treatment paradigm known as *reality therapy*. Reality therapy is based on the beliefs that quality of life is largely related to one's own choices, and at the core of all emotional problems is a problematic relationship. Glasser explained that the common denominator in problematic relationships is the need to control others and their choices. In order to improve relationships, one must strive to let go of the need to control someone else's choices and instead focus on making more positive choices for oneself, especially in how one relates with others.[9]

The reality therapist's job is to help clients discover what choices they have made that may have caused issues, and then counsel them to make better, healthier choices in the future. Although a discussion of the family of origin and the etiology of the client's dysfunction is considered in the course of therapy, Glasser chooses to focus on the present choices that clients are making. In a nutshell, instead of being past-focused, reality therapy is present-focused, guiding clients to make better choices, thereby improving their future.[10]

A family is basically a group of individuals making choices. Each family member's choices affect the function of not only the family unit but also the other members of the family on an individual level. Families in conflict need to consider the choices they make both as a unit as well as individuals. To improve the health and function of the family, each member must take responsibility for their own choices that may contribute to the current dynamics of the family—especially in times of conflict—and commit to making different, healthier choices going forward. By each member focusing on their own choices, it decreases the tension caused when there is an attempt to control the choices of fellow family members. Control is key. Controlling one's own choices and allowing others to do the same leads to more satisfactory relationships and greater life satisfaction overall.

Practical Application

The theories and techniques presented in this book have been invaluable in improving the health and function of our own families. To illustrate this point, we have included a couple of examples of how we have put these ideas into action in the following text boxes.

The Math Problem

My daughter was in 5th grade when she told me she intensely disliked math as it was boring. As a result, she paid less and less attention and eventually zoned out. I had just begun my training in Glasser's reality therapy and decided to put it to the test. I asked her if she was able to control the fact that she had to take the math class. Her response was that she could not. I then invited her to think about what she did have control over and could change. She thought about it and came up with an idea to help her stay alert in class. She decided she would try doodling on her page while her teacher lectured. We agreed that she would try it for a week and see what happened. I explained that if that did not work, we could rethink other strategies until she found one that worked for her. Happily, she found that the doodling paid off. She was able to stay more alert, pay more attention and eventually focus. We spoke about it and she understood that the only thing she was able to control and change was herself, and by changing her own behavior, she had improved her relationship with math, including improving her grade!

This is a simple illustration that speaks to the power of not expecting circumstances or others to change, as well as not trying to control things and others. One can only be proactive about one's own choices.

—Angela Mitakidis

The Unmade Bed

Several years ago, I began to make my bed every morning after I got up. It was not a habit I had learned during childhood, but it was one that I decided to teach myself. I have always struggled with insomnia and in my reading up on the subject I learned that for some people, something as simple as walking into a neatly made bed each night, helps to alleviate some of the precursors for an insomniac episode. Deciding it was worth a try, I began to develop the habit and found that it does in fact help me to begin to relax. I have also found it helps improve my morning attitude, which tends to be on the grumpy side naturally, to start my day having accomplished a task before I leave my bedroom.

My husband is a pilot and spends many nights in hotels where there is daily maid service. As such, he rarely has to make his own bed. Additionally, he couldn't care less what state his bed is in when he's ready to end the day. He usually sleeps like the dead.

This is where the trouble started. As I began to form my own bed making habit, my husband felt no need to do likewise. He wasn't opposed to having the bed made each day, but it wasn't important to him either. As the days and weeks went on, I began to become frustrated when he failed to make the bed if he was the last one up. For the life of me, I couldn't understand why he just didn't do as I asked and make the bed. I started to allow that simple frustration to cloud my entire day. "If he would only make the stupid bed, I wouldn't be grouchy in the morning," played on loop in my brain.

One day I was talking with a friend about a fight she had had with her husband. As we were chatting I asked her to consider whether she was attempting to truly find a compromise, or merely wanted her husband to acquiesce to her wishes. Furthermore, I advised her to examine her own choices and how those choices were in control of her emotions and subsequent actions. After all, the only person she could control was herself.

And that's when it dawned on me: I was choosing to be upset because my husband refused to allow me to control his behavior. Upon this epiphany, the revelation of my path toward a better morning attitude appeared. Should my husband be the last one up and fail to make the bed, I would simply go make it and keep my big mouth shut. I could choose to be bitter and foment unhappiness, or I could choose to realize that if it was important to me, I should have no problem making the bed after my husband got up. It was as simple as that.

Happily, I can report that it no longer angers me when my husband doesn't make the bed. In fact, as I have changed my behavior, he has started to make the bed most of the time. And I'm a little easier to be around in the morning.

—Shannon Brown

Our Roadmap

As we begin to delve into the complexities involved in effective management of conflict within families, we will operate with the following assumptions influenced in great part by the combined works of both Bowen and Glasser:

- Human behavior operates within a social system.
- A human being's first social system is their family of origin.
- The family is, in turn, a subsystem of a larger social system (community, country, world).
- The family is influenced by the relationships, rules and roles among its individual members, as well as by the relationship, rules and roles within the larger systems (laws or social mores).
- Change in one member of the family will affect the whole family, and in turn, the larger system.

**Families are a unit made up of individual parts.
When dealing with conflict within the family,
there must be consideration given to each
family member's role in the situation.**

Chapter 3

A Cycle for Every Family

"It's the circle of life, And it moves us all
Through despair and hope, Through faith and love
Till we find our place, On the path unwinding
In the circle, The circle of life."

—"Circle of Life," *The Lion King*

Life is like riding a bicycle. To keep your balance, you
must keep moving.

—Albert Einstein

The Family Life Cycle

In our earlier chapter, "Defining Family" (see Ch. 1), we highlighted
how diverse and in a constant state of evolution a family can be. Society
is increasingly embracing new family structures outside of the traditional
nuclear family. However, there continues to be a fairly consistent life cycle
regardless of the type of family structure. To borrow a term from *The Lion
King*, it's a "circle" of family.

We refer to the family we were born into as the family of origin,
whether biological or otherwise. At birth, we generally join a family whose
cycle is already in motion. Take a firstborn, for instance: The birth of the
first child is the triggering point for a new stage of development within a
family. The new parents move from being a pair to a three-person unit.
At the same time, the position of their parents moves from parents to

grandparents. With a second addition to the family, the firstborn becomes a sibling as well as the eldest child, and so on and so forth. The cycle continues to spin, as does one's position within it.

Simply put, the family is in constant motion as it grows, reorganizes, grows some more, reorganizes again and grows some more. With that, it moves through time. Though families are unique and there may be exceptions and variations, there are some generalizations that can be made about the typical life cycle of any family.

There is much research and literature on the family life cycle stages and what they look like. Within each of the stages a unique set of conflicts may arise. Awareness of what to expect in each stage will go a long way in preempting possible areas of conflict. Through personal experience, we have summarized the family life cycle into 7 general stages:

1. Coupling
2. Formation
3. Expansion
4. Child Rearing
5. Launching
6. Empty Nest
7. The Golden Years

The 7 Stages of the Family Life Cycle

In the interest of brevity, the terminology refers to an historically traditional family of husband, wife and their biological children. However, it is important to bear in mind that any family will be able to identify with most of the life cycle stages. Depending on the family structure, some stages will be prominent, others less so; some will be complex, some simple, and for some families a particular stage may not be applicable. We will touch on a few of those variations later. We believe these to be a workable description of the stages most families will cycle through within their lifetimes.

1. Coupling

The commencement point of a family is the coming together of two independent, adult individuals. These individuals decide to make a commitment to one another, joining their lives from that day forward. This can be smooth and exciting, turbulent and daunting, or any combination thereof.

While the commitment itself is key in the coupling stage, there are other factors at play. A hallmark of adulthood is the move from dependence and interdependence on family to independence. The coupling process requires that individuals move from independence back to interdependence, this time on the individual's chosen life partner. Having become accustomed to a reliance on oneself, and providing solely for one's own needs and desires, a person in the coupling stage now has a partner who needs to be factored into the equation.

To build intimacy, each individual must learn to allow the other the space to facilitate the meeting of both needs and desires. Furthermore, there must be a willingness to support one's partner in meeting their own—and sometimes unique—needs and desires. Blending, therefore, begins from the get-go, with the blending of each person's separate, independent life into that of the newly formed partnership. Partners in this stage are learning to accommodate each other's needs, interests, personality and temperament with the goal being to form a cohesive unit.

Furthermore, there is a need to move allegiance from one's family of origin to that of the nascent partnership. This does not imply that one is abandoning connections and cultural traditions of the family of origin, but it does mean that those connections and traditions are thoughtfully integrated into one's new family upon mutual understanding and agreement of both partners. In any event, decision-making for the most part moves from independent decision-making to consultation and collaboration, then agreement, before it can be adopted willingly and peacefully by the couple as a unit. Sometimes circumstances will call for putting the needs of a partner over the needs of one's own family of origin. This can be a lengthy process and continues throughout the life cycle.

2. Formation

Following the decision to move from singledom to coupledom, the new couple must define for themselves what it means to form a family and how the couple as a single unit will now start to build its own culture and traditions. We call this the formation stage. As discussed above, collaboration is key here. There are many factors at play in this stage of family development, and several questions must be asked and answered to facilitate a healthy familial foundation:

- How do we deal with finances?
- How will we allocate our time together?
- How will we deal with each other's needs for independence?
- How involved will our family of origins be in our new family?
- How do we navigate difficulties we face?
- How much of our old individual lives will we incorporate into our new shared life (activities, friendships, even furniture)?
- How will we handle holidays, family of origin traditions, vacations?

The importance of discussing all of the above cannot be underscored enough. Since the couple will have to decide whether they will incorporate the traditions they grew up with into their own family unit—and if so, which ones and to what degree—it is crucial for each partner to tread sensitively, respectfully and unselfishly in these discussions. The reason for this is that some traditions are so much a part of the family of origin's culture, it is more a definitive value of the family's identity than a mere ritual the family carries out on special holidays. When one begins to touch on values and identities, without sensitivity, respect and generosity, conflict can easily arise. These types of conflicts are often the first internal familial conflicts that must be dealt with.

Once the couple has mutually agreed upon which traditions stemming from their families of origin will and will not be incorporated into their new family, the first external familial conflict is often waiting in the wings. The new family will have to be strong in the face of possible opposition from members of their respective families of origin. It can be incredibly difficult for parents to watch their grown children choose not to incorporate values and traditions they feel should be so ingrained in their child that they would never abandon them. When this happens, a united front is essential. Failure to support one another in these types of conflicts with families of origin may sow the seeds of discontent before the new family has a chance to get off the ground. Couples may find themselves alternating between both families of origin to celebrate holidays together, and sometimes couples decide to create their own new way of celebrating.

These are just a few of the issues that young families face. The goal of this stage of family development is for the couple to agree upon their definition of family and outline the basic ground rules for the operations of their newly formed family.

In time, the couple will move organically into a rhythm of habits, routines, activities and interests. There is no exact time frame within which this happens. Sometimes couples talk about the first year of marriage being the most difficult. This is not always the case. One of us (Angela) experienced a relatively smooth first few years of marriage and then transitioned into a challenging phase after the birth of her first child. The other (Shannon) had a more difficult first few years of marriage, but a slightly less fretful transition into parenthood. Each family will have their own difficult times, but hopefully their amiable times will more than compensate for those stressful periods.

Whether simple or complicated, the formation stage is a time when a couple in a collaborative partnership motivated by love, friendship and commitment becomes a fully formed family, complete with its own values, goals and purpose.

3. Expansion

"You're going to have a baby!" This phrase often signifies the arrival of the next stage of family development: the welcoming of children. This period of expansion, particularly in its early phase, can be more difficult than the coupling stage as the couple is required to reallocate their responsibilities and take on new ones.

If and when a family decides to have children (biological or adoptive), a reorganization of time, priorities, flexibility and leisure time will be necessary. In fact, everyone in the family, including extended family, acquires a new role in this stage. The couple become parents; the parents of the couple, grandparents. Siblings become aunts and uncles; a niece or nephew is now a cousin, and so forth. Accommodation, patience and tolerance is key in this phase as everyone adapts to their new roles.

The concept of becoming a parent can be extremely daunting for some people well before the baby arrives. In addition, there are a number of things families must negotiate:

- The needs of the dependent child must be added to the already existing needs of the family.

- There is often less flexibility in scheduling due to the needs of children such as feeding schedules, naps, etc.
- Couples find themselves needing to renegotiate their personal needs and wants, including their intimacy. It can be difficult to find any time alone, particularly in the infancy stage.
- The family's financial situation must be re-evaluated with the additional costs of raising children.
- The couple must decide how to handle childcare. If both parents continue to work, they must plan for the care of the child, be it with the help of an extended family member, such as a grandparent, or a nonfamily provider.

In addition to these negotiations, family of origin issues may resurface in the expansion phase as the newly minted grandparents often expect to spend more time with the new family than they did before the arrival of children. It may become necessary for the couple to renegotiate some of the things they originally dealt with during the coupling and formation stages, as well as reassert boundaries with their families of origin.

First-time parents may also find themselves facing issues of parenting style differences, particularly when it comes to expectations and discipline. In addition, this stage necessitates that the family constantly evolve as the needs of children change as they get older. This signifies the beginning of the next life cycle stage.

4. Child-Rearing

There is an endless amount of research and literature for parents entering the child-rearing stage. Advice can be sourced on a plethora of topics concerning babies, toddlers and the elementary school years. There are plenty of books providing information starting with the selection of a suitable birth plan, moving on to toilet training, introducing a new sibling, discipline, parenting styles and so forth. However, when it comes to parenting the adolescent there are fewer readily available resources. Due to the seeming dearth of books on adolescence, and our belief that it is a crucial time in the life of an individual and family, we have elected to dedicate a deeper discussion of adolescence in a subsequent chapter (see Ch. 6).

With a seemingly endless supply of wisdom on child-rearing, it seems as if this would be one of the easiest cycles to navigate. That could not be further from the truth. Each stage of a child's development offers a new challenge to a family. As such, parents find themselves constantly adapting and changing the way their family functions.

The need for constant adaptation is stressful. Additionally, couples often find themselves discovering things about each other and their respective childhoods that they did not already know. These new revelations can at times cause conflict. Differing ideas about discipline, monetary allocation, chores for the kids, are all potential land mines. We humans have a tendency as well towards falling into old habits, like those learned in our family of origin, that may not be acceptable to our partner. Couple all of this with the knowledge that in the latter part of the child-rearing stage there may be some feelings of midlife crisis for one or both parents. At the same time an adolescent is jockeying for premature independence, and so this otherwise happy family becomes a powder keg trying to avoid the lit match lying beside it.

Recognition of the unique challenges during this stage of a family's life is imperative for mitigating and/or resolving conflict. Thankfully, while this phase is fraught with peril, it is also filled with an untold potential for joy. Remembering that potential is key to navigating this stage in a positive way.

5. Launching

The progression from child to adolescent to young adult varies, but is generally held to be from 12 to 24.[1] In this stage of launching, the parent-child relationship transitions to a more adult-to-adult relationship as the young adult prepares to leave the family of origin.

The goal of most families is to raise functioning adults that transition into their newfound adulthood smoothly and successfully. The process of launching essentially means separating from one's family of origin and assuming responsibility for oneself. This separation may include a place of residence, financial independence, responsibility for actions, emotional independence, marriage and so forth.

Ideally, this is also the point at which there is a shift in the relationship dynamic between parents and their children. The relationship should move from the authoritative one of past stages, into a more mentee-mentor relationship. This is accomplished as parents relinquish their need to control their children's decisions and instead embrace a new advisory role. For some families this is easy; for others it is a very difficult time fraught with painful conflict.

This stage of the family life cycle can also be the most varied of all, depending on the family's culture, economic stability, health and social circumstances. Not all young adults leave home at the age of 18. Some leave only when they marry. Others may marry and bring their partner into the family home. Still others may marry and bring parents into the new couple's marital home. Economic considerations may also play a part in the timing and ease of transition into this stage. For example, young adults saddled with large debt for continuing their education often find themselves needing to return home as they attempt to begin their careers. These are known as boomerang children.[2]

A solid understanding of cultural diversity is essential, especially when assisting families in conflict in this stage. Family members should be encouraged to share their cultural beliefs and traditions when seeking assistance with any type of family conflict. For example, in South Africa, 18 is not the traditional age for leaving home as it is in the US; children usually leave home when they marry, move in with their significant other or are able to support themselves financially.

The age at which individuals reach adulthood is also somewhat fluid. In the past, it was not uncommon to marry at a very young age, even in adolescence. Today, however, there has been an increase in the average age of adulthood and marriage. The rising cost of education and basic living expenses, the acceptance of marriage at later ages, the risks associated with STDs and sexual experimentation, fear of divorce, the willingness of families to allow children to continue residing at home may all be contributing factors to this delay in reaching adulthood.

Societal changes and cultural differences also contribute to the definition of adulthood. It stands to reason that the acceptance of women in the workplace translates into the ability for women to be more financially independent than in past centuries. This also allows women more flexibility in lifestyle choice, meaning where to live, when to get married or to remain altogether single. No matter the timeline for launch, the vast majority of children eventually leave home, thus triggering initiation of a new stage in the life cycle of the family.

6. Empty Nest

When children start to leave the family home, the family begins to contract as the couple goes from living with children to being on their own again. Depending on the relationship, the couple may find itself having to realign as a unit and become reacquainted as a couple.

The importance of working on one's marriage throughout each stage of the family life cycle cannot be overemphasized. It is not unusual for a relatively happily married couple to reach the empty nest stage only to realize that what they thought was a happy, intimate marriage has instead become a peaceful coexistence, more like friends or roommates than husband and wife.

The absence of the children, who naturally consumed much of the couple's time and attention, may inadvertently shine a light on a marriage that has become platonic and devoid of intimacy. As soon as the couple becomes aware of this, it is imperative that they seek ways to reignite not only their commitment to doing life together but also the intimacy they experienced in their early years.

As stressful as this stage may be for some couples trying to rediscover what it means to be a family of two, it may conversely be a time of financial relief and freedom. The empty nesters typically experience fewer demands on their finances and time, allowing them to enjoy life afresh.

The continuation of the midlife crisis period into the empty nest must be kept in mind, especially if one spouse was the primary or stay-at-home parent. Oftentimes that spouse must now find a way to fill their time. Some may choose to re-enter careers previously put on hold, begin to look for a new career or opportunity, or retire.

While this stage may usher in feelings of sadness related to the lack of the physical presence of a couple's children, most couples don't have long to wait before a family expansion begins anew—an expansion that brings with it the blessing that is grandparenthood.

7. The Golden Years

The years in which a couple is advancing in age are sometimes fondly referred to as the golden years. They may well be golden for a couple who remains healthy, active and financially self-sufficient. However, due to changes in employment status, income, health, death of a spouse and inability to care for oneself, a couple may find this stage of life extremely challenging. Children and grandchildren often become caregivers and/ or providers for their parents/grandparents. These forms of role reversal can be emotionally and psychologically challenging to all involved. The so-called sandwich generation is experienced in families where a couple may be caring for adult children as well as aging parents.[3]

The increasing needs of aging parents may cause stress between their adult children and their partners. The adult siblings must now negotiate both the needs of their own family at home and the needs of their parents. Sadly, this often leads to the fracturing of the sibling relationship, but this fracture is far from inevitable. We address the topic of aging in depth in a subsequent chapter (see Ch. 7), including some techniques to help navigate the specific stressors of elder care.

Modified Family Life Cycle Stages

While the majority of families today are made up of the traditional two-parent heterosexual households, they are not the only type of family found in our 21st century society as discussed earlier. In recent years, the number of nontraditional families continues to increase.

Divorced and blended families, single-parent households, multi-generational living arrangements, same-sex families and families of choice are a few of the typical variants from the traditional family model. Despite their differing makeup, the family life cycle is still applicable to these families, although they may face some unique challenges. What follows is a look at a few of these potential differences.

Divorce and Remarriage

Divorce and remarriage are two of the most common variants from the traditional family model. Initially, divorce may push a family into a contraction phase as one larger household becomes two smaller ones. The dissolution of the original family requires a renegotiation of roles, particularly for the parents, and a reallocation of both financial and human resources. Additionally, the children must come to terms with having roles in two separate families or within a new blended family containing stepsiblings, including differing rules and expectations between households.

The amiability of the parental split greatly affects every member of the original family. When the former partners can agree to co-parent and keep their differences away from their children, the transition is usually easier. When there is animosity and protracted battles over such things as custody and discipline, areas of conflict are certain to arise immediately. All of this is a choice on the part of the splitting couple. They can choose how to end the relationship in a way that will not add to the pain their children are inevitably going to face. Whether they mean to or not, parents can make the separation far more painful for the children than it needs to be. Parents must find a way to pull themselves together and learn to manage inevitable conflicts in a manner that will not end up in their children's laps. We have seen far too many couples argue over finances and how much or little needs to be spent on the children. If only these couples understood that money they think they are saving today will be needed for child therapy tomorrow! Parents need to spend more time and money at the separation stage to ensure they lay a healthy and workable foundation to co-parent their children going forward.

In addition, it is critical that parents understand that while they have moved on from one another, their children will never move on from them. The couple might no longer be husband, wife or partner; however, their role of mom and/or dad will never change. That fact must be made clear to the couple's children. Too often children internalize the animosity between divorcing parents and some even take on the blame for the dissolution of their family. It is imperative that the separating couple make it clear to their children that the parents alone are responsible for the divorce and there was nothing the children could have done to keep it from happening. Failure to do so can have serious ramifications for the children during their childhood and well into adulthood, including in their own relationships.

Regardless of the circumstances of the marital dissolution, it is a time of transition and may require a detour from the normal progression of the life cycle stages. We encourage parents to make healthy, thoughtful choices in this detour. For couples who do not have children, separating from one another in a way that upholds respect and human dignity cannot be emphasized enough. This is vital for emotional closure, long-term well-being and a healthy start to a new relationship in the future.

While divorce can cause a detour, remarriage can signify a return to an earlier stage in the family life cycle. Remarriage may propel a family into an expansion stage as they embrace stepparents, step siblings and half siblings. This newly blended family faces several hurdles as it begins its own life cycle, negotiating rules, cultures and traditions for itself, just as newly married couples must. Additionally, the new family must navigate issues such as finances, parenting styles, visitations. The blending of families is not easy, and all family members need to exercise patience and tolerance in order for the new family to bond and begin functioning as their own healthy family unit.

Single Parenthood

There can be no denying that single-parenthood rates are on the rise. In 2018, approximately 35% of children in the US were being raised in single-parent families.[4]

Discussion of the various psychological theories regarding children raised in single-parent homes is beyond the purview of this text. However, it is worth pointing out that children in single-parent families can flourish and succeed just as well as children raised by both parents. In our opinion, it is the meeting of needs (physical, social, emotional, educational, relational) that is vitally important to raising healthy, happy and productive members of society. Being raised in a single-parent home may come with its own challenges, but those challenges can be overcome by finding alternative ways to provide for needs that are more readily met in a two-parent home.

One particular obstacle single-parent households face is the increased risk of poverty. A 2014 study found a direct correlation between poverty and single-parent families.[5] Whether one is the cause of the other is still up for debate, but there remains a correlation between marital status and poverty. In this case, financial stability and security will necessarily be impacted. And where stability is impacted, there is risk of added stress and conflict within a family.

Same-Sex Families

By and large, two-parent, same-sex families experience the same stages of the family life cycle as the traditional family. However, some of these families may have faced unique challenges along the way. It is not uncommon for each partner in the relationship to have independently struggled with embracing their sexuality, coming out to their friends and family, and then facing prejudices. When starting a family of their own, many of these same prejudices and challenges rear their ugly heads. While the landscape is changing rapidly, especially in the legal field as evidenced by the Supreme Court's ruling in 2015 (*Obergefell* v. *Hodges*) guaranteeing the right of gay/lesbian partners to marry, many of these individuals face criticism and rejection in the social arena, both with their extended families and in society at large.

In cases of adoption, or even post-divorce custody, it is not uncommon for homosexual individuals to hide their sexuality from ex-spouses, family members, government agencies and/or the courts, out of fear of losing custody or refusal to grant them an adoption.

Awareness of the common challenges and detours that those in a same-sex family may face is important for those of us desiring to assist such families in conflict. The ability to identify those speed bumps and detours, and how they may affect a family in crisis, is an invaluable skill for the management and resolution of the unique conflicts these families may face.

Role Reversal

The reversal of roles within a family is not uncommon, especially as parents age. While we will discuss aging in depth in a subsequent chapter (see Ch. 7), we felt it was important to acknowledge how role reversal can affect the life cycle of a family. Below is an example of how this can happen.

The Panini Press

A few years ago, my father battled stage IV melanoma. To further complicate matters, he also had back surgery and suffered a stroke in the midst of his cancer treatment. As a result, my father was slowly robbed of his independence. Sadly, it did not end there. A couple of years later my mother tore her rotator cuff and required surgery to repair it. She was therefore unable to drive or tend to my father. I stepped in and became their primary caregiver and taxi driver.

While my parents were beginning to move into a period of role reversal, my husband and I were solidly in the child-rearing stage, quickly approaching the launch stage. Balancing the care needs of my parents, my children and my marriage felt impossible. It seemed as if I was in a constant state of letting someone down. I simply could not be all things to all people, but I tried my best to do just that.

For the most part I was okay, but I did have my moments. One of them came when my husband, children and I traveled out of town for a family vacation with my husband's entire family. Prior to my departure I spent days working through my parents' various appointments and setting up rides for them, ensuring they had groceries before I left, coordinating with my brother to cover the necessities and lining up friends to serve in my stead should unanticipated needs arise. I left feeling fairly confident that their needs would be covered.

Initially, everything seemed to be going smoothly until the second week of our vacation. I began to get texts and calls about small issues and my stress levels began to rise. By the end of that week, while the entire family was out for a walk, I got a frantic call from my parents that a major issue had arisen. My elaborate system had failed, and I felt caught between my need to be with my family on vacation and my need to be home caring for my parents.

While on a call with them, I fell behind the family on one of our walks. I thought I was by myself so I turned around and allowed myself a couple of exasperated sighs and frustrated tears. I was wiping my eyes as I turned back around to catch up with the family only to realize my father-in-law had stopped and waited for me. He said nothing about my tears. Instead he smiled at me and then very succinctly summed up the situation. He said, "I know this is a hard stage of life to be in. You're stuck between two sets of people that need you—your children and us parents. We're the bread and you're the filling. Welcome to the panini press." I cannot begin to tell you how grateful I am to him for his kind words. His acknowledgment of my situation brought relief. In that moment, I knew that I wasn't alone, my stress had been validated and we were going to survive this. As I find myself quickly approaching the empty nest phase, I know that my days in the panini press are numbered. That knowledge is bittersweet, but it is all part of the family life cycle. Someday it will be my children's turn to be the filling in the family panini. I hope that I can offer as much support and encouragement to them as my father-in-law did me that July afternoon.

—Shannon Brown

Another example of role reversal is when a child comforts a parent who is going through a crisis such as divorce or illness. In this situation, the child takes on the role of comforter, which is usually the role of a parent. These types of role reversals can be common in the life of any family. Can you think of a time when you have had to reverse roles with a member of your own family?

Other Family Types

The traditional family and the other variations discussed are just a few of the different types of families found in society. Grandparent-led families, polygamous families and multigenerational families are a few other family types. It behooves one to be aware that each of these situations come with its own challenges. On the flipside, they also provide unique rewards. For example, in a grandparent-led family the learning curve may not be as steep for the adults when it comes to child-rearing practices.

These families' life cycles may look a little different, but they must contend with many of the same transitions as their more traditional counterparts and therefore many of the same conflicts.

Conclusion

No matter the outward appearance of a family, there is no denying that each family has a life and cycle of its own. Awareness of this cyclical nature is incredibly advantageous when trudging through familial conflict, be it your own or that of a family you are working with. The ability to identify which stage a family is currently in the midst of can be the basis for the formation of an action plan when attempting to mitigate a conflict.

While the principles presented here are universally applicable, it is important to bear in mind that there is no right way to progress through the cycle. Families are so varied and unique that each family has the freedom to modify the stages described. These modifications may include unique challenges, rapid advancement, the skipping of a stage or even U-turns within a family's cycle. The important thing to bear in mind is that the goal is to produce happy, well-functioning families, no matter where they fall on the life cycle wheel.

Families, like other natural systems, have a life cycle. Gaining awareness of the specific stage in the life cycle of a family can help family members understand the dynamics of conflict in that stage.

Part II:
Genesis of Family Conflict

Chapter 4

The Nature of Family Conflict

Conflict is an expressed struggle between at least two interdependent parties who perceive incompatible goals, scarce rewards and interference from the other party in achieving their goals.

—Ronald B. Adler, *Interplay: The Process of Interpersonal Communication*

Humans have finally found something they can agree on: conflict. Not only is it inevitable, it is most probable.

—Angela Mitakidis

Definitions of Conflict and Family Conflict

All humans experience conflict. Conflict is like the common cold—easily acquired and mostly passes after a while. How it passes is in the individual's hands. When managed effectively, conflict can be a powerful opportunity for growth; when managed ineffectively, it has the capacity to destroy lives.

If conflict is so common, and therefore familiar, why is it usually perceived only in a negative light? Is there a possibility that conflict can be constructive, positive and healthy?

Singapore author, mediator and leadership consultant, Dr. John Ng, writes in his book *Dim Sum for the Family* that the absence of conflict is not a guarantee of relational wellness.[1] We agree with his position. We have seen individuals and families sweep unresolved issues under the proverbial carpet for various reasons: poor communication skills, fear, the desire to save face or avoid further conflict, and so forth. Over time, however, these issues compound until one day someone explodes. Finding a way back from that may be precarious and sadly often proves impossible.

It is rather disconcerting that conflict, something human beings are so familiar with, is usually not managed effectively. We will discuss how conflict can be constructive, but it is important to bear in mind that if the positive elements of conflict are not recognized and issues are not effectively managed, the opportunity for resolution is lost and quickly slips down a destructive path. Ng states that irresolvable conflicts can lead to bitterness, perpetual bad relationships, emotional burnout, depression. Therefore, hurt parties should aim to recover from conflict.[2]

In our experience, we have seen a progressive emergence of conflict before it becomes full-blown. It typically starts when a human being perceives one or more needs at a specific moment in time. The individual then attempts to satisfy a need. If that need is not satisfied immediately, or within a reasonable time frame, frustration ensues. When the individual is seeking the fulfillment of a need from another human being, things become more complicated. If the need is not fulfilled, frustration quickly turns to anger and conflict between the individuals develops. Note that we use the word *perceives*. It makes no difference to the individual in need whether it is a real need or a perceived need. In the individual's mind, there is a need that must be satisfied and if it is not, distress ensues.

Although this is a simplistic explanation of why humans experience conflict, consider how it can play out in real life. Take someone getting ready for a special date who remembers her sister has a perfect necklace to complete her outfit. She approaches her sister who refuses to let her wear the necklace. The need is to look pretty for the date. The interference of the sister by not helping meet this need causes frustration. If refusal persists, the individual going on a date moves from being frustrated to outright angry. Conflict takes on a life of its own and the sisters end up in a situation of escalating conflict. We have all experienced situations like this. Now imagine the conflict and damage that can occur when the unmet need is to feel valued and/or loved. Far too often, failure to mitigate small fissures, like those involving a necklace, leads to larger fractures, like not feeling loved enough to have a need met. It can swallow a relationship —and potentially a family—whole.

Despite the typical view that conflict is destructive, we believe that conflict, when handled appropriately, can be constructive. This is not as novel a concept as it may seem. After all, most of us are familiar with the concept of "make-up sex." Let us take a closer look at how conflict can be both destructive and constructive.

Destructive Conflict

Unchecked anger and unresolved conflict have the potential to delve into a downward spiral very quickly. If a requested need remains unfulfilled, it will lead to conflict. If conflict, in turn, is met with ineffective communication, heightened emotions, pride, anger, denial and a desire to sweep things under the carpet, that conflict has the potential to become destructive. In the family environment where family members may expect to be immediately forgiven of anything and everything, a small conflict can become a nuclear disaster in the blink of an eye.

Authors Jack Balswick and Judith Balswick use the terms *denial* and *displacement* to describe destructive ways to deal with conflict. Denial is self-explanatory: One or both parties ignore their conflict and continue their lives as though nothing happened. Displacement is described as taking out frustrations on weaker family members—in other words, projecting anger onto a family member who will in all likelihood not retaliate.[3] Considering the variety of personality types within a family, it is easy to understand how readily displacement can happen. It is crucial to be aware of family members who are less likely to be assertive. Those family members may bear the brunt of the effects of conflict, which in turn impacts how they handle their own conflicts in the future.

Authors Craig Runde and Tim Flanagan state that the basic nature of human beings is to evade those experiences that are painful or even unpleasant.[4] We can all agree that we would rather not be in conflict because of its unpleasantness. However, in order to live authentic and healthy lives, individuals must find a way to be more constructively engaged in the process of conflict as well as in the resolution of it. Ignoring conflict is like allowing a wound to fester. As the pressure builds and builds, disastrous consequences are inevitable.

Attacking the other person is another way in which conflict can quickly become destructive. An attack is often the result of the desire to win rather than resolve conflict peacefully.[5] We can take it one level further to say that the desire to win emanates from a reluctance to be seen as wrong. Being wrong is embarrassing, defeating and can lead to shame. One can therefore understand why winning can be so important. The problem, however, is that winning a small battle in a destructive manner can lead to a more serious loss at the end of the day if the conflict is unresolved: the loss of the relationship.

Destructive ways of handling conflict such as unchecked anger, denial, blaming, attacking and the desire to win at any cost only promote chaos and dysfunctional relationships. Thankfully, there is a better way to handle conflict, a way in which relationships can build strength that can then be leaned upon when the next battle surfaces.

Constructive Conflict

Constructively handling conflict is the optimal way to preserve and even enhance our relationships. Anger that is effectively de-escalated, and conflict that is dealt with in a timely manner, leads to a shift in direction—a shift from decline into that of ascent. Think in terms of moving from the valley to the top of the mountain where the view is clear and the air crisp. People who have experienced constructive conflict, even once, tend to remember the path to the mountaintop. Even in the worst conflict, when they are found in the deepest of the darkest of valleys, they will remember the first time they got to the glorious mountaintop and found victory over what could have mired them forever in the pit of the valley.

Constructive management and communication turn conflict into opportunity. Conflict can serve as a catalyst for the creation of new ideas for workable solutions. Individuals who disagree in a calmer and more respectful manner are able to get the creative brain into working mode, which leads to productive brainstorming of problem-solving. It also mutualizes the problem, making it a common issue to resolve together. Constructive conflict management techniques promote authentic and healthy responses that serve to calm, not inflame, emotions, and ultimately lead to healing contentious relationships.

We believe the most important technique in the journey towards constructive conflict is effective communication. This may appear obvious, but it is astounding to see how frequently individuals communicate poorly, if they communicate at all. We will focus on effective conflict management techniques and communication skills more thoroughly in subsequent chapters. Suffice it to say, constructive approaches to conflict should come on the wings of respect, calm discussion and loving confrontation.

Levels of Conflict

It can be disheartening to realize how quickly conflict can spiral out of control. An awareness of this is important in order to avoid the escalation of conflict beyond manageability. To assist in understanding the progression of a conflict, we have summarized the "Levels of Conflict" model by Speed Leas, a consultant and conflict resolution contributor of Duke Divinity School's Alban Institute:[6]

Level 1: Problem to Solve

Signs: Real disagreement, conflicting values and needs. Problem, not person-oriented.

Emotions: Short-lived, controlled anger. A little uncomfortable in the presence of the other(s).

Language: Open sharing of information, clear, specific.

Goals: Solving the problem. Win/win outcome.

Actions: Discussion. Collaboration.

Level 2: Disagreement

Signs: Differing perspectives are more strongly defined and positioned. Begin personalizing issues, shrewdness, calculation.

Emotions: Distrust, cautious, less mixing with the other(s).

Language: Selective holdback of information on both sides.

Goals: Face-saving, to come out looking good but not yet win/lose conflict.

Actions: Real effort to reach a win/win solution.

Level 3: Contest

Signs: Win/lose dynamics. Resist peace overtures. View opposition as the enemy.

Emotions: Cannot stand the presence of the other(s). Not willing to share feelings.

Language: Personal attacks. Distortion of information. "You always..."; "I never..." Attribute diabolical motives to the other(s).

Goals: Shifts from self-protection to winning. Objectives/issues get more complex/less focused.

Actions: Ripe for mediation. Compromise.

Level 4: Fight or Flight

Signs: Shifts from winning to getting rid of the other(s). Don't believe that the other(s) can change nor want them to change.

Emotions: Cold, self-righteous. Does not wish to speak to the other(s) anymore.

Language: Unwilling to listen or accept contrary information. Talk of principles not issues.

Goals: No longer care about winning. Wish to eliminate opposition or escape from the situation.

Actions: Final level for third party mediation. High probability of split.

Level 5: Intractable Conflict

Signs: Issues no longer clear. Personalities have become the issue. Conflict is now unmanageable. See the other(s) as harmful to society.

Emotions: Obsessed with attaining goals at all costs. Vindictive. Lose objectivity and control of emotion.

Language: Skewed to achieve a goal. Use words that destroy the reputation of the other(s).

Goals: Annihilate offending person(s).

Actions: Resolution is no longer possible. Damage control through a higher authority, for example, law enforcement or the court.

The Food Feud: A Hypothetical Escalation of Conflict

Angela and Shannon decided to go to lunch after a hard day of editing their forthcoming bestseller. Angela, being of Greek heritage, suggested they eat at her favorite Greek restaurant. Shannon, having grown up in Alaska, preferred to go to the local seafood restaurant. They were obviously at an impasse.

They began to discuss their options and made a case for each of their preferences. Angela mentioned all the lovely salads available at her choice, while Shannon regaled her with tales of grilled halibut steaks, in attempts to persuade the other into agreeing to her choice. At this point they were still fairly cordial, but were both digging their heels in, escalating the situation.

The argument grew heated. "But we ALWAYS have Greek food," exclaimed Shannon, while Angela countered, "You NEVER want to agree with me, about anything." They both privately thought about using a coin to help them choose, but neither wanted to let the other win.

"Fine, if we can't even agree on where to eat, then why are we still friends?" shouted Angela. Shannon raged in response, "You always have to be right! Plus, you know I can't eat cheese. You don't care that feta cheese will make me suffer. I'm honestly better off without you." The women were so loud that they drew a crowd of spectators, blocking any chance to escape the conflict.

The argument continued and escalated to the point where the two friends declared each other enemies. Shannon decided to burn down the Greek restaurant so Angela could never eat there again. Angela did likewise to the seafood establishment. Now the entire town lives without either restaurant. Both women are serving life sentences in, thankfully, two different federal penitentiaries.

As humorous as the highlighted fictional vignette may sound, it is not far-fetched but grounded in human nature. Consider the case of a business partnership gone awry. Is it not difficult to imagine an ousted partner burning down the warehouse in retaliation? What about the case of an employee who is continually sidelined for promotion because of race, ethnicity, gender? Is it not possible the employee may be so enraged that the boss's tires are slashed one evening? These examples sound extreme, but they have all happened.

Conflict does not usually start at that level, Level 3. Instead, it begins at the beginning, Level 1. Constructive resolution remains possible throughout Levels 1, 2 and 3. However, Level 3 ought to be considered the final red flag before a conflict is about to go down an intractable path. The progression from Levels 3 through 5 can be rapid, and conflicting parties would do well not to let their conflict escalate beyond Level 3. The language used in each level is a good clue as to how the conflict is progressing. Hopefully, after reading this book, you will keep from reaching Levels 4 and 5 in your own relationships, and even help others to do likewise.

Differences Between Familial Conflict and Nonfamilial Conflict

Now that we have discussed conflict in general, let us turn the focus to family conflict specifically. Is conflict with a family member different from conflict with a non family member? If so, then how and why do they differ? We believe there are a number of factors that explain the differences and why family conflicts are often more serious in nature.

"We hurt the ones we love" is a well-known phrase. This idea is bred out of the intimate nature of family life. Our family members are usually the people who know us best—our thoughts, feelings, dreams. They are also familiar with our weaknesses. In healthy, well-functioning families, there is an expectation of unconditional love and understanding, and that forgiveness for trespasses will be freely given. We feel safe expressing ourselves to our families and are willing to be vulnerable.

While this type of intimacy is often the goal of a healthy family, it can become a double-edged sword when conflict arises with a family member; they know how to hit us where it hurts and are often unafraid to go there. This explains why the more intimately one knows a family member, the more intense or heated an argument may become, and the more destructive the conflict.

With a non family member, an individual may be more careful and respectful in how they respond to conflict or the potential of it. Nonfamily members are often unaware of the other person's strengths and weaknesses. This lack of intimacy assists in keeping the focus on the conflict itself, instead of allowing it to become more personal in nature. It is easier to keep your eye on the prize of resolving conflict when dealing with a non-family member because the personal stakes are often lower. The conflict becomes about the issue, not the person.

Constructive conflict can also serve as a way to get to know a person more deeply and more intimately. This is true whether dealing with a family member or a non-family member. However, we believe that constructive conflict is of particular value in family settings. After all, if one never has a disagreement with a spouse, one may never know what their spouse likes and dislikes, what pushes buttons and triggers offense, and what makes them feel valued and loved. A loving relationship can carry conflict in a way that brings a new level of care to avoid hurtful words and behaviors, and in turn increases respect for one another.

Whether conflict involves family or non-family members, the importance of good communication skills cannot be overstated. While communication must happen to resolve either non-family or family conflict, lack of communication wreaks particular havoc within a family. This lack of communication is often referred to as stonewalling. When family members go radio silent in the midst of conflict, such behavior can be incredibly destructive as it removes any pathway to resolution. As family members are tied together in ways non-family members are not, the effects of broken relationships over unresolved conflict can lead to broken families. Typically, the stakes are not as high in unresolved nonfamilial conflict. Many nonfamilial conflicts end when the conflicting parties decide to part ways without resolving their issue. It may have an effect on those two individuals, but it rarely leads to the dissolution of an entire family unit.

Conflict is difficult no matter who is in conflict, but family conflict is often more difficult to mitigate and comes with a higher price should resolution be unattainable. The existence of children within families serves to further magnify the dire consequences of unresolved, or destructively handled, conflict. As more and more families in conflict opt for the dissolution of family instead of resolution, children are having to face difficult situations and circumstances.

Conclusion

In this chapter we identified the nature of family conflict, discussed constructive and destructive conflict, explained levels of conflict, and examined some key differences between conflict outside of and conflict within a family. In our next chapter we will examine neurological mechanisms involved in conflict.

Understanding conflict and learning how to deal with it constructively can be the difference between building up or tearing down a family.

Chapter 5
The Amygdala Hijack

Pardon me, my amygdala is showing.

—Shannon Brown

What if we told you that you have been hijacked many times without realizing it? The portion of your brain that plays a key role in the processing of emotions is called the amygdala. It has a pesky habit of taking over all our systems during times of stress, thereby controlling our decision-making process.

This phenomenon is commonly referred to as an "amygdala hijack."[1] Although a discussion on neuroscience is beyond the purview of this book, it may be helpful to gain a brief understanding of what happens to a person experiencing a high stress situation, whether from a physical or emotional threat or attack. In the midst of any conflict, including one involving family, it is possible that a simple verbal attack can cause the brain to embark on a journey of self-preservation; this is what happens in the brain when one feels threatened in some way. The brain does not distinguish between a physical attack and a psychological/emotional attack. The threatening stimulus of a touch, sight or sound quickly sends a fear signal to the thalamus at the center of the brain and then travels a short distance from the thalamus to the amygdala (the primary center of emotional and memory functions), at the base of the brain. Once the amygdala is activated, it sends millions of signals to all parts of the body to prepare for fight, flight or freeze in an effort to protect itself. What follows thereafter is a chain reaction. Adrenal glands are signaled and begin secreting corti-sol, adrenaline and noradrenaline. These hormonal surges in turn cause the heart to pump blood more forcefully to the muscles in preparation to defend oneself.[2] Ever wonder why you might feel a little shaky or unsteady when you are angry or afraid? Your amygdala is attempting a coup!

Individuals may vary in response to a threat, but once the amygdala is triggered, it takes over control of those areas of the body (for example, the muscles) that need to be mobilized to protect itself. The focus is there-fore on survival, not executive functioning. The prefrontal cortex, the center of executive functioning, is temporarily hijacked by the amygdala to focus on the part of the brain that will mobilize the body to defend itself. What follows is that one may appear to be unreasonable or irrational, simply because one is in survival mode, not thinking mode.

This is a completely normal physiological response to a perceived threat. We deliberately use the word *perceived* to underscore that the threat does not have to be real for the body to react irrationally. The threat merely needs to be perceived by the individual for the chain of events to ensue. Making judgments on the legitimacy of a person's reaction is rarely beneficial to resolving conflict. Instead, recognizing the reality of the consequences of the perceived threat, a.k.a. "the hijack," can be the first step in the journey to resolution. Conflicting parties will be wasting precious time trying to reason with one another at a time when the amyg-dala hijack is taking place. We recommend that one waits until the parties have decompressed to a degree that executive functioning returns and a logical discussion can be pursued.

The effects of the above referenced hormones are quite remarkable when activated. For example, when cortisol is released in response to stress and low blood glucose concentration, it increases blood sugar and aids in the metabolism of fat, protein and carbohydrates. Adrenaline increases blood flow to muscles, output of the heart, pupil dilation and blood sugar.

Noradrenaline increases arousal and alertness, and focuses attention; heart rate and blood pressure increase, as does restlessness and anxiety.

The activation of these hormones is a good thing when in physical danger since the body is prepared to deal with an attack, and to do so quickly. However, the frequency of threats has profound effects on our bodies. Elevated cortisol causes loss of neurons in the prefrontal cortex (executive functioning), kills neurons in the hippocampus (short-term memory) and decreases serotonin ("happy" hormone). Unfortunately, it can have a detrimental effect on the ability to resolve emotional conflict in a logical manner. This additional influx of these hormones and continued release during protracted conflict can have dire consequences on a person's physical health.

The good news in all of this? You do not have to let your amygdala win! You usually just have to wait it out. There are effective ways to deal with the physical effects of the hijack. You can literally run the extra energy off; decrease your heart rate and respiration with deep breathing; take a moment to step away (pause) from the stress-inducing situation. Whatever it takes, you need to remind yourself that your amygdala is not the boss of you! Sadly, many people do not take the time to allow their body to return to a less aroused state and end up acting rashly. That failure to mitigate an amygdala hijack often results in conflict and even broken relationships. Hopefully, now that you understand how the amygdala works, you will not let it hijack your entire life. You may not be able to keep the amygdala from rearing its ugly head in the face of stress, but you have the power to keep it from doing any long-term damage to your physical, emotional and relational health.

From Ogre to Princess

At the tender age of 20 I married my college sweetheart and then moved thousands of miles away from all I knew to the great state of Texas. My new husband and I found ourselves learning to be a family with no one to help us. It was no easy task. Our transition to married life was definitely more difficult for us than the transition to parenthood. I am grateful we had six years to get our act together before we had kids!

You see, I was not very good at handling stress, and consequently anger—mine or anyone else's. It took me many, many years, and countless failures, before I came to the point where I manage anger in a positive manner more often than in a negative one. (Some of these anger management techniques are discussed in Ch. 12).

To complicate my issues with stress, I am not a fan of hot weather, and Texas has more than its fair share of heat. I tend to be grouchy, overly sensitive and easily overwhelmed in a stressful situation. Combine this character trait with the inferno that is a Texas summer, bake it until late August, and you have a cake of C4 primed to explode. Sounds like a great addition to the marital buffet, doesn't it?

The first full summer we were married was a doozy. Much to my chagrin, I did little to control myself when faced with stress, and my amygdala took full advantage of this weakness. When the hijack happened, it was not flight or freeze I chose—it was fight. Something as small as a pair of dirty underwear peeking its offending head out of the laundry hamper was enough for me to launch into dressing my husband down for being a slob. Poor guy, he thought he married Princess Fiona, not the ogre known as Shrek!

My hot temper began to create a larger problem: unhappiness and dissatisfaction. It was at this point I realized that I had to change my own behavior, starting with the basics of how

I handled stress. It was time to put my amygdala back in its place, instead of letting it run roughshod over my life and my marriage. The journey has been difficult but worth every step of the way. I doubt my husband remembers me doing it now, but when I first embarked on reigning in my impulses, I used to verbally acknowledge the physical and emotional sensations triggered by my amygdala. If I began to react rashly to a minor stressor, I would stop for just a moment, say, "Pardon me, my amygdala is showing," take a deep breath and then continue on in a calmer, more rational manner. This small change had a huge, positive effect on my life, my marriage and eventually the lives of my children.

So, the next time you feel like your amygdala is trying to take over, I encourage you to take a moment to acknowledge it, pause to allow yourself to regain your equilibrium and then assess the situation that brought about your upset. I would hazard a guess that most of the time, you can stop a conflict in its tracks without uttering a single word.

—Shannon Brown

Stress causes our bodies to enter a state of arousal that we must manage to de-escalate before attempting to constructively resolve conflict.

Chapter 6

Adolescence

Too often we forget that discipline really means to teach,
not to punish. A disciple is a student, not a recipient of
behavioral consequences.

—Daniel J. Siegel and Tina Payne Bryson, *The
Whole Brain Child: 12 Revolutionary Strategies
to Nurture Your Child's Developing Mind*

Adolescence is arguably the most difficult time period of a person's life, and therefore deserves a little extra attention. Sandwiched between childhood and adulthood, it is a minefield on which many battles are fought: responsibility vs. irresponsibility, dependence vs. independence, rationality vs. emotionality. As an adult, it is easy to attribute all of these struggles to a lack of maturity and an overflow of hormonally produced emotion.

We often discount adolescents and their points of view, and this can lead to conflict within a family. The long-held belief that teenagers are solely at the whim of their hormones has been challenged in recent years due to advances in technology, specifically MRI scans of the brain. As we continue to find keys to resolving family conflict, it is important to look at the period of adolescence through a fresh lens and hopefully gain a new perspective on how and why adolescents behave the way they do.

We hope that by doing so, parents may begin to view the adolescent years as a time of creativity and great possibilities, when their children are the least fearful of taking risks to develop themselves and explore their creativity. This is a time of life in which inventors and gifted individuals are identified, and it is our hope that we turn the narrative around and begin to empower and encourage our adolescents with excitement about the possibilities awaiting them.

The importance of the mentoring role of parents in this stage of life cannot be emphasized enough. Parents should make every effort to bring enthusiasm and positivity into the lives of their teens, and not wish these years away. Parents should focus less on the executive functioning tasks (which do not fully develop until their mid-late twenties) such as organization, neatness and order, and more on innovation, excitement and energy. Parents who shift from a teaching role to that of a mentoring role during adolescence may be more successful in fostering a positive relationship with their teens, thereby forging a better relationship into their adult years as well.

Imagine a family in which everyone experiences a more peaceful transition to adulthood, instead of constant conflict during the teen years. This is possible, especially when parents begin to view adolescence in a positive light instead of a negative one, and focus on what their child is doing right instead of what they are doing wrong. If one shines a spotlight on the positive, the negative grows dim.

The Fact and Fiction of Adolescence

Before we begin to look at the recent research on the adolescent brain and how it functions, it is important to confront some of our own currently held beliefs about adolescents and their behavior:

1. **Fiction:** *Raging hormones cause teenagers to lose their minds.* While it may at times appear as if teenagers are controlled merely by their hormones, this is not the total picture. Research presented later in this chapter demonstrates there is important work going on in

the brain of an adolescent. Hormones, as it turns out, play a much smaller part than once thought. The tendency towards emotional outbursts, once thought to be caused by hormones, is in fact a by-product of the natural maturation of the brain. **Fact:** *Dramatic neurological changes cause normal developmental changes in the levels of teenagers' emotions and hormones.*

2. **Fiction:** *"Let's just get through the teen years!"* Many parents, and even some teenagers themselves, believe that adolescence is merely an unpleasant time of life that must be endured. The teenage years are believed to be a period of intense irrationality and irritability that must be soldiered through in order to reach adulthood. However, the reality is the adolescent brain is learning to move from an emotional response center to a more rational one as the portion of the brain in control develops from the amygdala region into the frontal lobe (responsible for reasoning and decision-making; executive functioning). At the same time, the brain is going through an intense period of pruning in which it decides which neural pathways need to stay and be strengthened, and which are no longer necessary. It is a "use it or lose it" process that we are wise to be mindful of as we approach ways to navigate conflict with teens. **Fact:** *It is profoundly important for teens to thrive in these adolescent years and therefore equally important that neither parents nor teens wish these years away.*

3. **Fiction:** *The goal of teens is to be totally independent of their parents.* It may be true that most teens feel this way at times. However, total independence is not the mark of adulthood, nor should it be the goal. Healthy adult relationships require a balance between the independence of the individual and their dependence on the person they are in relationship with. Adolescents are in the process of finding interdependence (a balance in their life between dependence and independence) that will impact their relationships for the rest of

their lives. They know they cannot be completely independent, but they no longer want to be wholly dependent upon their parents. It behooves parents to help their teens find this balance and honor their children's need to move from child to adult. At the same time, parents need to be mindful of the fact that adolescents are more dependent than they want to be, thus conflict often arises when parents assert their governing role. **Fact:** *Teens seek interdependence, not independence.*

4. **Fiction:** *Parents and teens do not desire the same things in life.* While living in Singapore, I (Angela) had the privilege of conducting parent-teen workshops in which one of the exercises was for teens and parents to privately rank a set of pictures depicting what they value from most important to least important. For example, there were pictures depicting self-esteem, confidence, wisdom, peace, contentment, long life, career, family, friendships, riches and reputation. Remarkably, the rankings selected by the group of teens and the group of parents were consistently similar; parents and teens selected family and peace as their top two values. Similarly, when conducting this same exercise in the US, the result was consistently the same. **Fact:** *Despite how it may appear on the surface, adolescents place greater value on their families and a desire for peace than we give them credit for; this is especially important to remember at times when conflict arises.*

A Peek Inside the Brain of Adolescents

It is imperative that as we continue a discussion of dealing with conflict in adolescents, and how it can be resolved, we look at recent research on the function of an adolescent brain. With the advance of MRI technology and its expanded use in the study of brain maturation, we now have some clues as to why adolescents appear to be driven more by their hormones and emotions than logic or reason.

A 10-year-long research study using MRI mapped the human brain of 13 healthy children and teens from childhood (around 5 years old) into the early 20s. The study showed that the brain continues to change into their early 20s with the frontal lobes, responsible for reasoning and problem solving, developing last. The brain matures from back to front and neural connections are pruned.[1]

These findings seem to indicate that some of that baffling adolescent behavior may be the result of neurobiology and not raging hormones. Prior to this study, it was assumed that brain development concluded, for the most part, by the teenage years. The decade-long study by researchers at the National Institute of Mental Health and the University of California Los Angeles (UCLA) shows that the "higher-order" brain centers, such as the frontal lobe, do not fully develop until young adulthood.[2]

The frontal lobe of the brain helps put the brakes on a desire for thrills and taking risks. The fact that this is the last area of the brain to develop fully may help to explain why adolescents often appear irrational and have difficulty employing logic in their decision-making. The frontal lobe controls judgment, organization, planning and strategizing—the very skills or rather lack thereof that get teens into trouble. This knowledge may help parents to rethink the expectation they put on their teens to have well-honed organizational skills or wise decision-making abilities before their brains are fully developed.

Scientists are still researching what accounts for this, but it may parallel a pruning process called "use it or lose it" that occurs early in life, around 18 months old, when it appears an overproduction of gray matter is followed by the loss of unused gray matter. Neural connections, or synapses, that get exercised are retained, while those that do not are lost. The research indicates a second pruning process occurring in the adolescent years.[3]

For example, if a teen is involved in music or sports or academics, those are the cells and connections that will be hardwired, while unused cells may be lost. Knowing what their teens' brains are going through, adolescence is a good time for parents to encourage kids to form healthy habits, shed bad ones and learn new skills. This may be easier said than done if teens are already averse to parental advice. Presenting the neuroscience information surrounding the formation of healthy habits may make it easier for adolescents to understand that what they perceive from their parents as judging and nagging is in fact an attempt to help them live long, healthy and fulfilling lives.

The lack of highly developed reasoning skills during the brain's adolescent pruning process also renders teens more vulnerable to risky behavior such as driving too fast and substance abuse. Many conflicts with teenagers are centered around risky, ill-advised behavior. While it can be easy to assign blame for these actions to faulty character, it is important to recognize that they are well within the range of normal behavior for an adolescent. That being said, it is also important for these behaviors to be addressed in a constructive manner that affirms them and encourages better choices in the future.

We have previously discussed the amygdala hijack, the neurological snowball effect of stress/anger in the brain. We encourage both parents and teens to get into deeper research of the neuroscience involved in conflict, especially in these developing years. This may go a long way in making concessions to one another, as well as allowing each family member the space to decompress and regroup. Understanding the biological underpinnings of adolescents' thoughts, speech and actions allows those involved in conflict with them to be more compassionate and understanding. While older teens may not be at the mercy of hormones, they are still in a period of significant physical maturation; therefore, it is of the utmost importance to demonstrate healthy ways to work through conflict. In effect, learning to resolve conflict during adolescence in a constructive way can lead to healthier relationships in adulthood due to good conflict resolution skills being hardwired into their brain. If they use it, they will not lose it.

The ESSENCE of Adolescence

We would be remiss not to mention the valuable work of Dr. Daniel J. Siegel in this area. Siegel is a clinical professor of psychiatry at the UCLA School of Medicine and executive director of the Mindsight Institute. He views puberty as a rich time of bodily and hormonal changes, as well as sexual awakening and maturation. Siegel considers dopamine, a neurotransmitter, an important component in this period. Dopamine is also the primary source of adrenaline, the hormone secreted by the adrenal glands in times of stress. Siegel explains that an increased dopamine release in the brain occurs in the teen years and causes an increased drive for reward. Enhanced dopamine release also occurs when one engages in risky activities. This increase in dopamine is a powerful incentive for teens to be risk-takers. Additionally, it causes them to be more susceptible to addictive behaviors.[4]

Siegel developed a model for discussing brain development in adolescence called "The ESSENCE of Adolescence." This model posits that development in adolescents occurs in four main areas: emotional, social, novel and creative. Employing the acronym ESSENCE, Siegel summarizes the common changes and needs of the adolescent brain during this period of life, as well as enumerating some of the challenges and benefits faced in each area.

Siegel breaks down ESSENCE as follows:[5]

ES (Emotional Spark): Teens experience an enhanced emotion generated from the subcortical areas of the brain overriding the cortical areas of reasoning.

>*Downside*: Intense emotion may rule the day with emotional storms and moodiness.

>*Upside*: A powerful passion to live life fully; to "capture" life.

SE (Social Engagement): This is the social programming of the brain. Teens start engaging more in peer relationships and less in parental relationships.

>*Downside*: If teens isolate themselves from adults and connect only with peers, the risk of increased impulsive and dangerous behavior can occur.

>*Upside*: The creation of supportive relationships, which research proves to be the best predictor of well-being, longevity and happiness throughout the lifespan.

N (Novelty Seeking): Circuit shifts in the brain's dopamine system create a drive for reward associated with thrilling and risky experiences.

>*Downside*: Risk-taking behavior can lead to injury and have serious legal consequences.

>*Upside*: The courage to leave the familiar, certain and safe home nest for the unfamiliar, uncertain, potentially unsafe world beyond.

CE (Creative Exploration): The brain develops conceptual thinking and abstract reasoning.

>*Downside*: The need to question and challenge the status quo can lead to identity crisis and conflict with authority figures.

>*Upside*: Problems can be approached with out-of-the-box strategies and innovation. Adolescents are open to change and eager to explore a spectrum of possibilities.

Siegel magnificently portrays how adolescents can go from ordinary to extraordinary, sometimes within the blink of an eye.[6] Awareness of these needs and shifts in the adolescent psyche is vital to helping teens and their families resolve conflict. Armed with this information, it is easier to find possible solutions to the most common difficulties that families with adolescent children face. It becomes of particular importance for caregivers/mediators as they formulate conflict resolution strategies for their clients or their own families.

Keys to Parent-Adolescent Interactions

Awareness of the unique struggles and biological workings during adolescence can assist parents and families in avoiding some conflicts. However, as previously discussed, prevention of conflict is not always possible, or even advantageous. When faced with conflict involving a teen, one's knowledge of the unique biological components of the adolescent brain, and its resulting tendency towards irrationality, is often the best place to start. Below is a helpful summary of key points to bear in mind when dealing with adolescents:

1. They *do* care about what parents think.
2. They are in a powerful stage of their lives in which courage and creativity peak. Mentoring a teen effectively and positively through these years is critical.
3. The lines of communication need to be open. Teens need to be received with positivity, and their views, opinions and ideas, respected and encouraged.
4. They are experiencing heightened emotions, both negative and positive. Parents should focus more on their teens when they are excited

than when they are down. Positive reinforcement will go a long way to make a teen feel validated.

5.   Teens need parents to be their mentors, not their teachers. We believe that by this age, parents have generally completed imparting the family values and positive behaviors to their teens. From this point forward, parents need to assist teens in their quest to find that interdependent balance. We encourage parents to embrace a healthy balance between parental control and their child's independence.

6.   Teens are seeking out role models and they want parents to fill that role. What parents *do* at this stage in an adolescent's life is more important than what they say.

Note to Parents

In our own experience with our teens, we have found them to need consistency, even if it does not look like it. What do we mean by that? We know teens are becoming more independent in this stage of life, but we also know that they are not fully developed as adults yet. They are emotionally inconsistent. Therefore, even though they verbalize and behave in a way that seems as though they are pushing the parent away, the reality is they need parents to be stable, consistent and not give way to the pushing of boundaries. They are subconsciously testing the one constant they have had all their lives, their parent/caregiver. Everything else in their life is changing so rapidly, they need to feel their one constant is not going to change.

The "dance" they're engaged in with their parents is one parents need to recognize and manage with the knowledge that their teen is simply testing the constant in their lives. They are not wanting to push parents out of their lives, but pushing to see if they will hold on, if their relationship really is constant, and if it will remain constant.

This is not a time for parents to let go, give up or express hopelessness. It is a time to stand firm, regardless of the circumstances their teens may find themselves in.

At the same time, this support needs to be accomplished alongside the knowledge that parents are still legally and financially responsible for their adolescent until the age of 18. Parents must therefore determine the best course of action to protect their child while allowing for more responsibility. Failure to act responsibly does not obviate the teen's need to learn responsibility. Parents will do well to seek wise counsel in this phase of the family life cycle and not try to navigate it alone. Parenting—especially of an adolescent—is definitely not for the faint of heart!

Instead of viewing adolescence as a negative period of time that must be endured until it is over, parents and teens should embrace the challenges it brings with hope and positivity. This is a time that has great potential for the strengthening of family bonds and a healthy transition from childhood to adulthood.

Chapter 7

Aging

We don't stop playing because we grow old. We grow old because we stop playing.

—George Bernard Shaw

The last century has brought unprecedented, rapid change. The advances in technology alone are likely to be challenging for the "Baby Boomer" generation. We have spent a fair amount of time discussing how the structure of families, particularly in the US, has changed. The prevalence of divorce, remarriage and blended families, as well as the impact of the 2008 economic downturn on the finances of families and even social ills such as drug addiction and HIV/AIDS that claim the lives of young parents (leaving behind orphans) all have a direct impact on the aging population.

The Baby Boomers, as our aging population is known, were born post-World War II between 1946 and 1964. The boom of births during those years made this generation, up until being overtaken by Millennials in 2019, the largest generational population in US history. As this population is now in, or entering, retirement, it is important to note that they are the first generation in the US to have a social security policy in place. Baby Boomers are not only experiencing the anticipated physical, cognitive, relational (particularly loss of loved ones) and psychosocial changes that aging has always brought on, they are also retiring later than their parents and facing unique challenges of the 21st century, including cultural and socioeconomic issues.

For all of the above reasons we felt it was important that we dedicate a chapter to discussion of this golden generation, the most unique population in the history of the US if not the world.

Dr. Myron F. Weiner, professor emeritus of psychiatry at the University of Texas Southwestern Medical Center in Dallas, Texas, states that family roles are changing and reversing rapidly in the 21st century as children begin caring for aging parents who are living longer than previous generations.[1] With this increase in lifespan, families face new challenges, most importantly caring for parents facing the various disabilities and impairments aging normally brings for much longer than ever before.[2]

One thing that has not changed is that the older the elderly become, the more dependent they become on others for care and support. The first group to be impacted by this need is the children of aging parents, followed by grandchildren and hired caregivers. Dr. Richard Caputo, Professor Emeritus at Yeshiva University, discusses research on a plethora of challenges facing the families of aging parents.[3] Some of these include:

- Lack of resources for elderly parents.
- Economic effects on families with aging household members.
- Quality of relationships between family caregivers and aging parents.
- Strong economic gains made by the Baby Boomers in the last 50 years due to the introduction of social security versus the strain on these gains due to 21st century family structures. Examples of these challenges include the raising of grandchildren and financial assistance for adult children who are struggling to gain financial independence.
- Types of affordable and/or available institutional care.

Socioeconomic Challenges

In the article "The Intersection of Economics and Family Status in Late Life: Implications for the Future," Elizabeth A. Kutza, formerly of Portland State University and the Institute on Aging, discusses her research on the economic factors impacting an aging family. Kutza's research shows the economic growth of today's retirees since the end of World War II. A contributory factor occurred as a result of President Roosevelt's 1935 Social Security Act (Old Age Survivors Insurance). Kutza goes on to explain the expansion of private pensions in the Baby Boomer generation, the decline in poverty in this generation and an overall sense of financial stability.[4]

Kutza's research also shows factors impacting family well-being:[5]

- The association between marital status and economic status, with the highest poverty rates residing in families of divorced, never married and/or widowed women.
- Participation of women in the labor force, resulting in the juggling of family responsibilities and work impacting well-being.
- Attempting to alleviate this juggling, women may seek part-time work, with resultant part-time retirement benefits.

Kutza maintains that the number of aging Americans is increasing rapidly. Apart from those already in retirement, it is estimated that the majority of Baby Boomers will enter young old age (60 to 75) between 2006 and 2030, and that in this time period the elderly population will be nearly twice as large as it was in 1998.[6]

Kutza also discusses economic factors impacting the aging population:[7]

- The decline in the American economy since the Baby Boomer era is resulting in lower incomes, less personal savings for retirement and lower retirement benefits.

- Changes in the law regarding the age of retirement have tax implications (taxable benefits, etc.).

- Changes in private pension plans: defined benefit plan vs. defined contribution plan (401K). A defined benefit plan is an annuity guaranteed over a lifetime and is based on monetary contributions and number of years worked, while a defined contribution plan is an annuity dependent only on monetary contributions.

- The collapse of major companies in the 1990s such as Enron resulted in massive pension fund losses.

- The economically at risk include people who have lacked access to education or had erratic work histories. Research shows these problems fall disproportionately on older people of color and women. This combination of race and gender in old age is referred to as "double jeopardy" in risk of financial security in later life.

The changing family structures in the 21st century have a considerable impact on our aging population. Where it used to be that one could rely on children to care for their parents as they aged, that is no longer the case in many families. Due to financial changes such as challenges with financial security and the possibility of providing financial support to their adult children, many elderly adults find themselves without the support they need in their retirement years. Social challenges such as single and/or grandparent-led parenting are another concern, as are physical challenges such as longer life span, increasing rates of heart disease and drug addiction, the rise in communicable diseases, including sexually transmitted ones, and other health issues. There has been a transition in how younger generations provide support for our aging population. Kutza confirms this by discussing a shift from economic support of the elderly to a more emotional and/or physical support in the form of caregiving.[8]

The Sandwich Generation

The population known as the sandwich generation is evident in society today with middle-aged adults who find themselves caught between caring for an aging parent while also still raising their own children (remember "The Panini Press" from Ch. 3). In the article "The Sandwich Generation is Growing, and So Are Their Responsibilities," John M. Campanola, a Financial Services Professional for New York Life, explains how the number of people caught in this situation of responsibility is rising rapidly, partly because couples are having children at a later age, and also because people are living longer. More and more adult children are returning home for various reasons such as financial and caregiving needs. This means that a person may remain in the sandwich generation for a long time.[9]

Given this scenario, it stands to reason that the sandwich generation needs to prepare adequately, both financially and emotionally, as well as gain coping skills for this added burden. Much of Campanola's article is about preparation for this stage, which entails getting acquainted with the various resources available in one's community and immediate circle. Campanola also underscores the need for parents to exercise self-care, and to ensure their own children are not neglected while caring for elderly parents. He offers encouragement to say, despite the fact that caring for children as well as aging parents is not easy, if families prepare in advance and employ available resources, it can be done successfully.[10]

This resonates strongly with us. Human beings are more resilient than we think. We have the innate ability to juggle a few balls at the same time, especially when we know how many we have and what they look like.

Boomerang Children

Boomerang children are adult children who return to their parental home later in life after having left at a younger age (typically 18 years old in the US). Financial difficulties adult children run into are the primary reason they return to the parental home. More and more children graduating from high school are recognizing the importance of tertiary education. If parents are unable to support them through their college years, adult children resort to loans which then have to be repaid after completion of their studies. Despite having obtained a degree, adult children are facing increasing competition in the marketplace and may have to settle for entry-level jobs that do not provide sufficient income to pay back loans and support themselves (and possibly a young and growing family). Temporarily returning to the parental home may be the only option for them.

The impact of this on aging parents who are now in their golden years is considerable. Of particular note is the dynamics at play within households where adult children return with a young family in tow. Elderly parents may find themselves not only supporting their adult children, but also enmeshed in the daily life of raising grandchildren. It can be a lot to manage successfully for everyone involved.

"The Talk"

We would like to introduce the concept of "The Talk." Often the first thing that springs to mind when the phrase "The Talk" comes up is the famously awkward discussion surrounding sexual development and procreation. We are in no way suggesting that you need to sit down with your parents and/or children to discuss sexual habits (although, with the rise in STDs in the geriatric community, a refresher may not be a bad idea). We believe it is of utmost importance to have an open and honest discussion of how a family will handle aging, whether it concerns yours, that of your parents, or of another family. Many families are reluctant to broach the topic of aging and the changes it brings until it is too late, which, sadly, often leads to conflict. Preparing ahead of time is the best way to avert these types of familial conflict. No matter the family structure, financial circumstances, caregiving abilities and any other socioeconomic factors impacting your family, it is crucial for the continued well-being of relationships within the family to plan a convenient and mutually agreeable time to meet and discuss what the golden years will look like.

There are two ways in which "The Talk" may take place. Firstly, and ideally, one should discuss what the golden years would look like for oneself. This will entail thinking and planning, as well as expression of one's desires. In other words, consider how you would like your own golden years to look, then put a plan in place to reach this ideal goal (as far as possible and as much as resources allow). Apart from planning ahead, an important component of this plan will be to express your desires to your spouse, children and/or extended family. This way, when the time comes, there will be fewer surprises and conflicts because there will be a blueprint to follow (perhaps with some adjustments or accommodations).

Another way in which "The Talk" may occur is among siblings and/ or extended family. Some elderly parents do not wish to discuss what will happen in their later years. They may not want to admit they are in the aging process. Denial is common, especially if they feel that by admitting they are aging and even ailing, they may lose their independence. For example, one of the most devastating moments for an elderly person is when they are no longer able to drive their car safely. Often, aging parents will not disclose this to their children in fear of loss of independence.

Whatever the circumstances, when parents are unwilling, or unable, to discuss their later years of life, it is imperative for siblings and/ or involved, extended family members to have "The Talk," with or without the aging parents. This will entail arranging a meeting to come up with a plan of how aging parents will be cared for in the event they become incapacitated.

Some of the issues that should be discussed are:

- What financial resources are available to the family?
- Which family member will take on the role of managing the finances of an incapacitated parent?
- Where and with whom will an ailing parent reside?
- If the decision is for the parent to transition to a caregiving facility, who will research the available facilities and determine which is the most appropriate for the parent and whether it falls within the affordability range of the family?
- In the event that there are inadequate resources available to aging parents, what will each family member contribute to the care of their parents?
- What will contributions look like? Will they be financial, in the form of caregiving, or taking the aging parent into one's own home?
- If elderly parents have not expressed their wishes regarding end of life, and in the event that a will has not been drafted, what plan is in place for the siblings and/or extended family members to cater the parent's end-of-life arrangements?

We cannot stress enough how important it is to have a plan in place to care for elderly family members as well as a plan for the end of life. When a parent begins to decline in health, children may find themselves in the throes of grieving the ailing parent and later on dealing with the grief of a parent who has passed. The last thing family members need or want is to be dealing with conflict with one another simply because a management plan was not in place beforehand.

Disagreements among siblings over the care and/or the end of life of a parent are not uncommon. In fact, these can be more traumatic and enduring than the grief experienced at the loss of the parent. How sad it would be to spend more time in conflict with siblings than in the normal and healthy process of grieving the loss of a loved one. We therefore encourage you to have "The Talk."

The Golden Years Can Be Golden

We would like to end this chapter on an encouraging and positive note, The National Institute on Aging published tips on aging, one of which was to encourage older adults to engage in enjoyable activities such as art classes and volunteering. It states that research has shown that older adults who engage in an active lifestyle are better prepared to cope with loss, stress and depression.[11]

Many of us have our own stories about family members, or elderly people we may know, who remain active and involved in their communities. They enjoy life and thrive in their golden years, versus those who have succumbed to the false notion that their old age has somehow rendered them incapable and of less value to society.

We would also like to underscore our belief that we have a joint responsibility toward those in their golden years, to afford them the ongoing opportunity to remain engaged with us and in their communities. We believe younger generations would do well to learn from the experiences and wisdom of this golden generation.

Grandma Bea

My grandmother, known to us all as Grandma Bea, was born in 1907. She lived in rural New Mexico in a dugout house. The property she grew up on is still in the family and while there is now a proper house, the original dugout as well as the tracks from the Santa Fe Trail that ran at the back of the property serve as reminders of a time gone by and as evidence of how much change we have seen in the last century.

When she was finished with her schooling, Grandma Bea worked as a teacher in a one-room schoolhouse. At the time she married my grandad, they had $8 to their name and left their wedding in a horse-drawn wagon. My grandparents made the journey to California during the Dust Bowl in search of work and eventually settled in the Central Valley of California. By the time of her passing in 2000 she had flown to both Hawaii and Alaska to visit us. What incredible change she experienced: from horse-drawn wagon to transoceanic flight.

Whenever I begin to feel overwhelmed by the change I see happening all around me, I remember my grandmother. Her entire world changed rapidly, yet she remained joyful and optimistic, embracing the new opportunities available to her. As I find myself aging, I hope that I optimistically accept the change around me, being mindful to hold onto the things from the past that hold value and letting go of what no longer serves me—just like my Grandma Bea taught me. Our elders are a treasure trove of experience and wisdom. May we honor them and their legacies.

—Shannon Brown

Understanding the unique aspects of aging, having open discussions about changing needs and relieving the fear of the unknown are imperative to mitigating and resolving conflict that may creep up on us with each passing year. In short, have "The Talk"!

Part III:
The Toolkit

Chapter 8

Family Conflict Management: Strategies and Techniques

Peace is not the absence of conflict, it is the ability to handle conflict by peaceful means.

—Ronald Reagan

There are many tools and techniques that can be employed to effectively manage conflict. We will begin to present the ones we believe are key. Before we explore specific tools, it is important to start at the beginning: the building of a basic foundation and progression upon which conflict can be managed in a constructive manner. This framework provides a good starting point when faced with conflict. It focuses on handling conflict in a positive manner and reaching a mutually beneficial outcome for conflicting parties. It is of particular value in family settings where the goal is to continue in a relationship following an upsetting incident. If we learn to utilize this ourselves, and then impart it to our children, imagine the positive impact it would have on our community and our society.

What follows is a framework upon which conflict can be constructively managed:

- **Plan**: Engaging in conflict can happen in the heat of the moment and catch a person off guard. Taking strategic pauses before continuing to engage in conflict is critical, especially if tempers have flared and there is little hope of de-escalating emotions in that moment. We will discuss how to take strategic pauses later; suffice to say, it is essential to employ tools to cool down, calm down and de-escalate anger before continuing with any discussions. The plan should entail agreeing to allow one another time and space to decompress and de-escalate heightened emotions. Also agree to a convenient time and a place to resume discussions in a calm and respectful manner when everyone has had a fair opportunity to de-stress. This could happen in an hour, the following day or even the following week if tempers are running exceedingly high. The key is not to engage in further discussions until everyone has decompressed.

- **Change Your Mindset**: A benefit of the planning step above is that the person moves from viewing conflict as purely negative to educational and restorative. When one understands that there is an issue to be discussed and resolved, parties are less inclined to view it as a combative conflict but rather as an important task to complete in order for progress to be made, especially when destructive emotions have been removed from the equation. Engaging in conflict then becomes more clinical, less emotionally charged, orderly and is eventually viewed as a potentially positive occurrence for a relationship.

- Begin to look for opportunities to view conflict as constructive and not destructive. For example, when a person sees that a conflict results in an opportunity to learn more about the other person, the conflict is not viewed negatively at all—you have just learned something more or new about the person you are in a relationship with! This could also be a wonderful opportunity to learn to communicate more effectively and approach one another more respectfully. This is when conflict becomes an opportunity for growth and turns into constructive conflict. A person recognizes that apart from one's own needs, the needs of the other person can and should also be met. In destructive conflict, the path each chooses is a self-centered one, aimed at meeting one's own needs with little regard for others.

- **Beware of Triangulating**: Ensure the conflict remains with the conflicting parties. When a person is angry at someone, it is very tempting to off-load on a third party. A person does this to garner support and sympathy, or just to let off steam. The result of this is that the third party may be pulled into a conflict that does not involve them personally and a triangle is formed. There is rarely a good outcome in such a situation for any of the parties, especially if the triangulating person is a family member. Once the conflict is resolved, a third party can be left out in the cold.

- **Seek Professional Assistance**: When a conflict becomes intractable in that a resolution seems highly unlikely, instead of giving up and adding hopelessness to the mix, agree to be open to seeking out professional help. This could be consulting a community elder, a pastor or layperson, a professional mediator, counselor, therapist, medical professional. Professionals have worked long and hard to equip themselves with the skills to be able to help others. Take full advantage of modern-day professions and skills that may mean the difference between a complete resolution or a complete breakup.

- **Adopt a Forgiving Nature**: We will speak about forgiveness more comprehensively later on. For now, suffice to say we feel strongly about the need to adopt, acquire, learn, seek—whatever way works best for you—to attain a spirit of forgiveness. We believe it is a vital ingredient for healthy family life. Forgiveness begins with a *willingness* to forgive, then progresses to a *decision* to forgive and, finally, to actually forgiving. Some people are more inclined than others to hold grudges, but everyone can learn to forgive. We have grappled with this and had to work hard to attain a willingness to forgive; now it comes more naturally, as does the decision to forgive. However, walking in that forgiveness is something we will continually need to strive for. Without a spirit of forgiveness, even one conflict in a family can be drawn out for years by parties who are unwilling to forgive. The impact on every member of the family is far-reaching and devastating.

These basic steps for managing conflict can be employed in any conflict, but are especially essential when dealing with conflict within a family. When conflict arises, a family that approaches the issue with a goal to reach as positive an outcome as possible usually comes out stronger on the other side.

Approaching conflict with a plan to reach a constructive resolution is a basic building block of a healthy family.

Chapter 9
Only You Can Choose

Life is made of choices. Remove your shoes or scrub the floor.

—Author Unknown

The Choices We Make

With the exception of our autonomic nervous system functions—among them, heart rate, digestion and respiratory rate—every action we take is the result of a choice. Even inaction is a choice. The same is true for our relationships and how we deal with conflict. This is more readily recognizable when it comes to a physical issue versus an emotional one. Below is an example of how one man's choice can make a difference in his life:

Ed is a 45-year-old married man and father to three children. Ed has started having trouble sleeping, so he goes to his physician. During the course of his appointment, his doctor makes several suggestions that may help him sleep better. First of all, Ed is about 50 pounds overweight and fairly inactive. His doctor tells him that if he commits to shedding his excess weight through diet and exercise, it is quite possible that his insomnia will resolve itself. Basically, Ed is given a choice: either commit to a healthier lifestyle and benefit from improved sleep, or do nothing and continue to suffer. Ed can choose to act or he can choose inaction. While the doctor offered advice and encouragement, the only person capable of making the decision and carrying it through is Ed. No one can force Ed to get up and move or, conversely, make him continue to sit around and neglect his health.

While Ed is dealing with a physical ailment, the same concept of choice can be applied to our relationships. We may wish people would behave in a certain manner or say things that are pleasing to us, but we cannot make them do it, nor should we try to. We simply cannot control the choices of others, just as they cannot control the choices we make.

This realization seems like a very fundamental idea, but it can be incredibly difficult to implement. It requires us to recognize that we are only in control of our own choices. It is human nature for us to desire to be in control, but we need to discern what we should be in control of and what we need to relinquish. This tendency to control can become problematic when we are in relationship with others. Even as parents, it is detrimental to our relationship with our children, especially as they enter the preteen years, to dictate their actions. They need to learn to choose good behaviors for themselves and the best way to do that is to be good role models ourselves.

Using this logic, one definition of a family could be a group of individuals making choices that affect the health and well-being of those they live in relationship with. Many conflicts within families are the result of members trying to control the choices of their fellow family members. Recognizing this dynamic is invaluable to the resolution of conflict within a family.

In his choice theory paradigm, Dr. William Glasser identifies five basic needs of humanity:

- Survival
- Love and belonging
- Power
- Freedom

- Fun

Glasser posits that every individual spends their life in pursuit of meeting these needs. It therefore stands to reason that when an individual's particular need is not met, the unmet need may cause frustration and eventually even conflict. This is especially true where a need is expected to be met by a fellow family member.[1]

Being cognizant of these needs may be very helpful in identifying the root cause of the conflict and formulating strategies to assist in its resolution. These five needs are briefly explained below.

Survival

This need is very basic and is found in every species on earth. The need for food, water and shelter may seem to be inconsequential when talking about family dynamics, however the truth is that it can play a role in family conflict. In fact, it can even be the precipitating cause of conflict:

Steve and Kayla have been married for 10 years and have two children, ages three and five. Steve has been working as a mechanic at a local car dealership for the past seven years. Kayla left her job at a diner to stay home and care for their children. Six months ago, Steve was laid off from his job and has yet to find new employment. The family was living paycheck to paycheck before the layoff and now finds themselves on the verge of homelessness. The stress of the situation has caused a fracture in their marriage. Steve is depressed and has given up on job hunting. Meanwhile, Kayla has started selling off anything of value to keep her family afloat and is frustrated that she is the only one addressing the family's needs. During this trying time, Steve and Kayla, who once enjoyed an amicable, happy and strong relationship, find themselves in a constant state of disagreement. They are continually at each other's throats and are discussing separating.

In the case of this family, the root cause of their conflict is fear over the inability to provide for their family the very basic necessities of life. Their survival is threatened. Should this couple manage to work through their issues, it may come to light that their struggle began to involve needs beyond those of survival, but there is no doubt that the survival need was the precipitating factor in their conflict. To remain connected they must choose to work together to find financial solvency. Steve must choose to continue searching for work, and Kayla must choose the best way to support him in his endeavor and determine if there is anything else she can do to help the situation, including pursuing work outside of their home.

Love and Belonging

The need for companionship can be found in many different species on earth. Canine species travel in packs, lions live in prides and even many fish live together in schools. Humans are no different and may be the species that need companionship more than any other on earth. We have the need to feel loved and to belong. In short, humans need to live in a relationship with other humans in order to feel satisfied with life.

This need to be loved and to belong is a driving force in family dynamics. When we feel accepted by those in our family, we feel satisfied and happy. When we feel judged and shunned, we experience anger and depression. Many conflicts within families begin when one or more members begin to feel as if they are no longer loved or belong in the family:

Edna has been married to Hank for 25 years. They raised three children and are now adjusting to life as empty nesters. During the course of their marriage, both Edna and Hank worked, but Edna bore the brunt of the responsibility for raising the children. She worked in the school system, which allowed her to work during the hours her children were at school.

Hank runs a very successful accounting firm. He was a loving father, but his job often required long work hours and his attendance at social functions after work hours to network and expand his client base. Edna occasionally joined him at these functions, but usually stayed home to tend to the children.

When the children graduated from high school and left for college, Edna continued to work at the school for a little while, but then realized that she had only kept that job to give her the flexibility to be around for her kids. Edna decides to retire from the school system and is contemplating going back to school to pursue a new career path. Meanwhile, Hank's business continues to flourish, requiring him to spend more time at the office than in previous years.

Edna begins to feel as if she no longer has a place in the world. Her children have successfully launched and no longer need her. The friends she made while working in the school are busy with their work and families. Hank is focused on his business and has not realized the distress his wife is feeling.

Edna feels adrift. She begins to resent the long hours her husband spends at work and assumes that Hank doesn't need her any longer. Her resentment turns to anger and that leads to bickering between herself and Hank. It has come to the point where neither Hank nor Edna feel as if their relationship can continue.

To the observer of this situation it is clear that the underlying issue is Edna's unmet need to feel loved. Furthermore, where she once satisfied her need for belonging in both her workplace and at home, she now finds nothing but loneliness. Because of this unmet need, Edna struggles to maintain a healthy relationship with her husband. She may have no awareness that this is the root cause of the conflict in her marriage, but nonetheless it must be addressed if she and Hank are to continue in relationship and resolve the conflicts that have arisen.

In order to restore her relationship with Hank, Edna must choose to find new ways to meet her need for love and belonging. Additionally, Hank must choose to help her feel loved and assist her in feeling she still belongs in their family. While he cannot control the choices Edna makes, he can assist her by being aware of and sensitive to her unmet need.

Families that are cognizant of each member's need for love and belonging tend to be happier, healthier and stronger. Members that choose to demonstrate love for one another help facilitate harmony and avoid large-scale conflict.

Power

Rare is the human that does not feel the need to have power or a solid sense of identity. The need for power can be seen in nearly all facets of society, be it in the school lunch table seating chart, the academic ranking of students, the scoreboard at a football game, a boardroom where each person is jockeying for a power position, or even at the dinner table as family members interact in a manner that clearly demonstrates a sense of power and/or identity.

This need may harbor the most potential for causing conflict within a family, particularly when examining the parent-child dynamic. Parents typically hold the power within a household. They are the older and wiser ones who are tasked with raising fully functioning adults. As such, it is easy to cross the line from exercising control over children that is necessary for their development to exercising control for the sake of demonstrating a more powerful position in the family pecking order:

Jason is the oldest of five children and has been given the task of mowing the lawn each week. His father, David, used to be the primary lawn mower, but has relinquished his duty in order to prepare his son for adulthood. Prior to his assumption of the chore, David spent a few weeks instructing Jason on the proper way to mow the lawn.

The first Saturday that Jason is responsible for the lawn mowing, he begins to mow while David tends to some inside chores. As Jason is finishing up the front yard, David comes out to check on his son. What he sees immediately upsets him. Jason has chosen to mow in a different pattern than David taught him. David immediately approaches his son and begins to tell him that he has done the mowing incorrectly. Jason becomes upset and begins to argue with his father that the lawn looks good this way. The father and son become locked in a heated argument. The argument leads to an evening of discord in the house.

In this scenario, David, the father, feels that he has lost power. His way of mowing the lawn, in his mind, is obviously the correct way. After all, he is the father and the head of the household. Jason, on the other hand, feels as if he found a better way to mow the yard, thereby providing him a way to exert a little bit of power of his own. These two warring needs for power led to a dispute.

Admittedly, this example is simplistic, but it illustrates the way the need for power can cause conflict. David wants to control Jason and balks at the idea of Jason asserting his own will. Jason wants to control his own actions and balks at David's attempt to assert his control over Jason. If these types of situations continue on a regular basis, it can devolve into family conflict, not just a small disagreement.

Both David and Jason can choose to assert themselves and their own ideas, without requiring the submission of the other party. They can agree to disagree and decide that either way of mowing the lawn is acceptable.

The choice is up to each individual party; neither can force the other into action. And as Jason continues to mature, David will have to continue to allow Jason to exert his own power over his own actions.

Freedom

The idea that we are in control of our own choices and destiny is the essence of the need for freedom. Humans have a deeply held desire to make decisions for themselves and be granted the freedom to live as they please. This need for freedom often rubs up against our need for community. In families this is often displayed by the need to make decisions in the best interest of the family unit as a whole, not just that of each family member.

There is a debate raging in the US today about how much freedom we are willing to relinquish to guarantee our safety and the safety of our society. We subject ourselves to security checks to buy firearms and to enter buildings and airplanes. In these instances, we realize that our need for freedom is trumped by the desire to live in a safe and secure community.

This same type of debate rages in families every day, be it the stubborn toddler that insists on touching a hot stove, the elementary school child that refuses to do their assigned homework or the mother that is tempted to lock herself in her bathroom in a desperate attempt for a little alone time. The need for freedom is challenged by the responsibilities and obligations of the need to survive (e.g., the toddler and the stove) and the need for love and belonging (e.g., mother in the bathroom). Couple that with competing needs for power, and the family itself is a powder keg of conflict ready to blow at any moment.

This becomes even more evident as children begin to age out of the home and take responsibility for themselves. The parents must balance the need for their child to survive with the child's need for their own freedom. Children must determine how to meet both their need to survive and their need for freedom:

Brian is 17 years old and has just bought a car of his own. It is Friday night and he is planning on going to the football game with a few friends. It is raining, but Brian is anxious to exercise his newfound freedom and drive himself to the game and then to a coffee shop afterward to hang out with his friends.

Jane, Brian's mother, is reluctant to let Brian go out into the rain in his new vehicle. It is the first time that Brian has driven his new car at night, and Jane is afraid that something bad may happen to Brian. In short, she is concerned for his safety and has a history of being slightly overprotective when it comes to her son.

Brian and Jane are at loggerheads when it comes to the situation. Neither is willing to budge, and an argument ensues. Brian accuses Jane of infringing upon his freedom, while Jane argues that she is his mother and as such has every right to deny his request to go out.

As an outsider, it is easy to see that Brian is attempting to meet his need for freedom, while Jane is attempting to exert her control (power) over Brian, while also fearing for his safety (survival). Neither may be aware of the internal struggle they are experiencing; they are merely focused on the argument. If this type of scenario continues to repeat itself, the two may fall into a pit of conflict that is difficult to climb out of.

Both Brian and Jane are only in control of their own choices. Brian must choose whether or not to exert his independence and go out against his mother's wishes, or acquiesce to her and stay in. Jane must choose whether to allow Brian some freedom or to continue to exert her power over him. They can only control their own choices, not the choices of the other. The choices they make will impact the quality of the relationship one way or another.

Fun

Life is hard. There is no arguing that point. Thankfully, one of our default needs as humans is the need for fun. Time and again, research proves the positive power of smiling, laughter and enjoyable activities. The need for fun is usually an easy one to meet. Sadly, when a family is in conflict, fun is usually the first need to be neglected. After all, it is difficult to immerse yourself in an activity that is supposed to bring joy when you are mired in conflict and/or hurt feelings:

Jay and Cindy had been married for five years. When they were newlyweds, they enjoyed golfing together. Neither one of them was particularly good at golf, but they loved being outside, walking together on the lush greens and laughing at each other's abysmal short game. It was the one thing they did routinely together as a couple.

About two years into their marriage, Jay received a promotion at work. With his new job title came new responsibilities and longer hours. Their time together golfing came to a halt. To add insult to injury, he would at times have to hit the golf course for work in a bid to expand his company's client base. While Jay continues to immerse himself in his work, Cindy begins to feel less important to Jay. Additionally, she resents the time he spends on the golf course without her. The combination of his long hours at work and her resentment begin to create friction in their marriage.

After one incredibly difficult week, Jay and Cindy decide they needed to spend some time together and have fun. Cindy calls their favorite course and reserves a tee time. As the couple work their way through the 18 holes, they find the game difficult to enjoy. Gone is the joy of past golf outings, in its place griping and criticism. Where they once laughed off bad shots, they now make cutting remarks.

Throughout their game both Jay and Cindy have been focused on other things. Cindy is mired in her resentment that Jay has been spending so much time at work and, due to his time on the golf course, has become a much better golfer than she. Meanwhile, Jay is distracted with thoughts of his job and is becoming increasingly irritated by Cindy's harsh demeanor and commentary on his golfing.

Their favorite activity, one that brought so much joy in the past, has become a drudgery. The fun is gone.

Jay and Cindy are headed for conflict. What may have begun as a discussion about a golf game may end with a discussion of priorities and dissatisfaction. Their attempt to meet their need for fun was sidelined by their growing discontent. Both Jay and Cindy bear responsibility for the unhappy circumstance they are in. Cindy could have chosen to focus only on the game at hand and enjoy time with her husband instead of giving into her resentment and thereby failing to have fun. Jay on the other hand had a choice of how to respond to Cindy's attitude. If this couple's need for fun is to be met, they must both choose to work at it until it becomes a fun activity again, or work at finding a new one that fulfills that need.

Choose Wisely

Elie Wiesel, the famed Holocaust survivor once said, "Ultimately, the only power to which man should aspire is that which he exercises over himself."[2]

This statement sums up the idea of choice theory and how it relates to relationships. We are incapable of controlling the choices of others; however, we can often, with a little self-reflection, ferret out the underlying reasons for conflict with those we are in relationship with. The concept of Glasser's basic needs is an invaluable tool in discerning the truth of conflict. When basic needs are not being met, conflict ensues.

In order for conflict to be resolved, and once the issue has been discovered, it is imperative that each person allow their cohort the freedom to choose their own actions. Any attempt to force the other party to make choices that you select for them will only serve to deepen the conflict and possibly damage the relationship irreparably. We must make our own choices and make them with the aim of turning toward one another.

Conflict often arises out of an unmet need such as survival, love and belonging, power, freedom or fun. Awareness of these needs, and the reality that we can only control our own choices—not the choices of others—can help resolve conflict.

Chapter 10

Name the Pain

We intuitively believe social and physical pain are radically different kinds of experiences, yet the way our brains treat them suggests that they are more similar than we imagine.

—Matthew D. Lieberman, *Social: Why Our Brains Are Wired to Connect*

Far too often in conflict we become entangled in a web of words. The words we speak and the words spoken to us bind together in a magnificent emotional trap, a trap easy to fall into and difficult to escape. Thankfully, there is a way to use words in a positive manner, even when in conflict.

We have discussed the damage that can be done to a relationship through harsh words. Sadly, our human nature—not to mention our hijacked amygdala—encourages us to lash out when we are angry. This emotional/physiological combination makes it difficult to break through the hurt and anger long enough to consider any feelings we have beyond these. It is even more difficult to consider the feelings of the other person. However, there is a tool we can employ to help us do just that. Validation, acknowledgment and affect labeling are some of the terms used by distinguished professionals in the field to teach this powerful de-escalation strategy. We call it "Name the Pain."

It is important to the conflict resolution process that those in conflict deal with the underlying emotions brought about by the circumstances. Naming the emotion experienced by us and vocalizing it *internally*, and naming the emotion of the person we are in conflict with and vocalizing it *externally*, is fairly self-explanatory. This means to actively name the emotions that are at play at any given time.

This interplay between naming an emotion and mitigating some of the physiological influence on one's behavior has been identified in a research study using functional MRI imaging. This study shows that the brain has the ability to de-escalate its physiological response to emotion once the said emotion has been labeled, thereby calming the amygdala and its temperamental nature.[1]

In other words, if we name the emotion we validate it—the effect of which serves to calm us sufficiently enough to bring us into a more rational frame of mind. This then allows us the ability to deal with and resolve conflict. Identifying our own feelings, validating them and then doing the same for the person we are in conflict with can foster a more amicable and empathetic environment in which to attempt to resolve our issues.

Let us look at an example of naming our own emotions, especially since we often experience more than one emotion when in the midst of conflict. The following text box is an example of how this is beneficial:

The Chores

A few years ago, my in-laws were about 30 minutes from arriving on my doorstep. I had been out running errands and left the kitchen cleanup to my kids. When I got home, the kitchen had not been touched and the kids were up in their rooms. Admittedly, I was very angry that they had not done as instructed. But anger was not the only emotion I was feeling. I was also feeling disrespected by their lack of obedience, and I was feeling fear—the fear of being judged deficient as a wife and mother by my husband's parents. I would love to tell you that I calmly admonished my kids and we all worked in the kitchen together. That's not exactly how I handled it. However, the fact that I became aware of all the feelings I was experiencing, and acknowledged that it was not only anger at play within me, helped calm me down and get the kitchen cleaned before our family arrived.

—Shannon Brown

A difficulty we face in resolving conflict is our tendency to stay focused on ourselves. We assign more importance to our own feelings than we do to those of the person we are in conflict with. Douglas E. Noll, author, attorney, mediator and peacemaker, suggests that when someone's emotions have escalated, we should not focus on the words spoken but on the emotion behind them.[2]

In other words, armed with the knowledge that naming and validating our own emotions is helpful, consider that naming and validating the emotions of our partner in conflict can be equally beneficial in de-escalating heightened emotions. Instead of focusing on the words spoken (especially words that are offensive), focus on what the person's emotions are at that moment. This helps us focus on the technique rather than the offense, and when we name the emotion, it serves to de-escalate the other person's emotions.

Affect labeling also promotes empathy. By putting ourselves in the shoes of the other person (physically and/or emotionally), we engage in a contemplation of what the other person might be feeling. Once we identify their feelings, we can then communicate our understanding of those feelings to them. The result of naming the pain is to acknowledge it and lessen its sting.

The text box that follows is an example of how naming another person's pain is beneficial:

The Car Wreck

A friend of mine was involved in a multiple car accident. Thankfully she was unhurt, however, she was understandably shocked and very emotional. Her adult daughter was the closest to her in proximity and so she called her to come to the scene of the accident and wait with her while things got sorted out. Once her daughter established that her mom was unhurt, she told her mom there was clearly no need for her to come out. My friend was upset with her daughter for her refusal to come to her aid.

A few days later, my friend and I met for dinner and she was still fuming. She vented for a good 20 minutes, all the while I was trying to console her and encourage her that her daughter loved her, but had just not been considerate at that moment, and so forth. Nothing seemed to calm her and she became more and more riled up as she told me about what happened.

I then remembered the "Name the Pain" technique and tried to guess at the root of her pain. At first, I said, "You're really angry," and she responded, "No, I'm not angry," and continued to vent. I then tried, "She hurt you by not demonstrating care when you needed it," and again she said, "no, that's not it," and continued to vent further.

My next attempt hit home. I said, "You felt abandoned by her." Immediately I saw her entire demeanor change before my eyes. Her shoulders relaxed, she sighed audibly, her frown disappeared and the relief in her voice was unmistakable when she responded in agreement. "Yes," she said, "I felt abandoned." That acknowledgement served to validate her deepest hurt and enabled her emotions to de-escalate and her to relax for the first time in days. The rest of the evening was upbeat and pleasant, a noticeable change from when our evening together began.

I learned a very valuable lesson about employing the "Name the Pain" technique. Even if you don't get it quite right at first, persevere and stay with it until you visibly see acknowledgement and validation of the other person's emotions. You'll know when you've finally decoded their feelings and will witness firsthand how powerful this tool can be.

—Angela Mitakidis

While we encourage the validation of the feelings of others, be mindful that this must be done cautiously. This technique should be studied in much more depth and applied with utmost sincerity, sensitivity and humility. It can happen that we turn an attempt to validate someone else's feelings into a projection of our own feelings. In spite of this, validation of others' feelings can still be done effectively; it just takes practice, practice and more practice.

We suggest using a simple strategy to effectively employ affect labeling using the acronym, NAME:

- **N (Notice)**: Take notice of your own feelings and put a name to them. This decreases your irrational brain reaction and increases rationality.

- **A (Acknowledge)**: Be sure to acknowledge the other person's emotions. Spend time decoding and naming the other person's feelings.

- **M (Mitigate)**: Lessen the gravity of yourself and your own feelings by removing them from the equation for a moment. Frame the labeling of the other person's affect through their own lens, not yours. In this context avoid *I* statements, which bring attention to your feelings, for example, "*I* feel you are angry." Instead, validate their feelings using *you* statements, for example, "*You* are angry." This is not to be confused with the active listening skill (that we will discuss later) of paraphrasing or summarizing. This is a technique aimed at naming emotions, not paraphrasing words.

- **E (Express empathy)**: Demonstrating to the other person that you are attempting to understand their perspective validates their feelings thereby allowing them to calm their own brain's irrational reaction to the conflict.

In summary, the first step to resolving a conflict is to recognize that you need to de-escalate emotions that could lead down a destructive path. The next step is to identify your emotions and those of the other person in conflict. After that, you need to express these in the form of affect labeling by naming the pain. This leads to empathy, which is a great way to demonstrate your desire for resolution and serves to alleviate the human tendency to resort to hurtful words and actions at the height of conflict. We cannot be caught in our own web if we keep from spinning it in the first place.

The ability to name our own feelings and the feelings of our conflict partner is an invaluable tool in de-escalating conflict.

Chapter II
The PEACE Toolkit

The peace we can aspire to then is not a harmonious
peace of the grave, nor a submissive peace of the slave,
but a hardworking peace of the brave.

—William Ury, *The Third Side: Why
We Fight and How We Can Stop*

PEACE

There is no denying that conflict can bring out the very worst in us.
We become selfish, critical, abrasive and defensive when we feel we are
being unfairly treated. When a marriage begins to become combative and
rife with conflict, it can become unbearable. A couple mired in conflict
must either decide to work together to resolve it and then continue in
their marriage, or decide to call it quits and dissolve their partnership.
Oftentimes couples see the dissolution of their marriage as the resolution
of their conflict. Unfortunately, that is not necessarily the case. Once in the
divorce courts, couples find themselves forced to deal with their conflict
and come to some kind of resolution in order for a divorce to be granted.
(Often the mediation process is used to this end.) What is clear, therefore,
is that there is no way to avoid facing the conflict. Our goal, and hopefully
yours as you read this book, is to keep families from finding themselves
in such dire conflict that the only way forward is divorce.

There are many techniques for dealing with conflict and managing
the interaction between those involved in a dispute. We have found the

PEACE toolkit to be most helpful in conflict resolution. The following strategic characteristics of peace, when applied consistently, can lead to a resolution that is workable and respectful to both parties:

- **P** (Pause)
- **E** (Esteem the Person)
- **A** (Actively Listen)
- **C** (Choose Your Battles)
- **E** (Equip Oneself)

P (Pause)

We have briefly touched on the importance of the pause, and we discuss it here in more depth as we believe this may be the best tool for de-escalating conflict. Couples in conflict often tend to behave in manners that increase frustration and anger levels. They blurt out harsh words to defend themselves from attack and by doing so only serve to escalate what is already a precarious discussion. Once conflict escalates, it becomes a runaway train. We all know how that ends.

Why does this happen? For one, we have hot buttons, and no one knows our hot buttons better than our family members. Having spent a considerable amount of time together, and assuming we know each other quite well, we are well-versed in how our partner ticks and thus how to get under their skin. This knowledge and the defensive tendencies humans possess when feeling wronged usually complicate the ability to resolve conflict.

When conflict arises, participants will do whatever it takes to defend themselves and above all will insist on being respected even in the midst of disrespecting the other participant in the conflict. That is observed in human nature. We cannot let go of our human dignity, nor should we be made to. Factoring in the amygdala hijack that we know occurs when we are stressed, we recommend a simple and effective tool to ensure the first words out of our mouths are not going to set that runaway train in motion: Take a strategic pause.

We refer to it as strategic because it is not something that comes naturally. One has to be intentional about acquiring and applying a tool of de-escalation before continuing discussions. The commencement of the conflict needs to be the red flag. It should trigger one's memory to pause before speaking. If one does not pause, what will come naturally is to hurl words of offense and hurt. Taking a pause before one speaks is the best first step in de-escalating the heightened emotions involved in any conflict (remember, the amygdala hijack is the mechanism behind this).

So, what does it mean to take a strategic pause? It means different things to different people. We have found that physically leaving the space where the conflict is occurring for a brief period is particularly beneficial. This allows those in conflict to spend a few moments away from one another, decreasing their own stress reaction, thereby allowing time for the heart rate to normalize in order to re-engage in a calmer manner.

The use of one's time during the pause varies from individual to individual and even from one conflict to another. The activities we have found most useful are those that help to expend the excess energy burst and/or decrease the heart rate acceleration that typically accompanies stress. Meditating, praying, doing breathing exercises, practicing mindfulness, and going for a walk around the block are all good ways to return equilibrium to the physical body.

Whatever the method that works best for each person, it is important to communicate to the other participant that one is not abandoning them or running away from the conflict. Being clear that one needs some time to allow anger to dissipate before continuing the conversation often encourages the other participant to do the same. It is also important to agree upon a set time to resume the discussion. This indicates a desire to return to each other and find a resolution. While it may elongate the time parties are in conflict, it is infinitely more productive and redemptive than staying in the heat of the discussion, thereby risking permanent damage to the relationship.

E (Esteem the Person)

Often the root cause of conflict escalation is one or both parties feeling disrespected or devalued. When we feel we are not being taken seriously, and our dignity is being devalued, we tend to become angry. This can create an impediment to resolving conflict constructively. It is important to ensure that all participants in the conflict feel valued and esteemed.

When one feels calmer and returns from a time of pause, communications can continue in a more respectful manner—a manner that esteems the person and maintains human dignity. Ground rules can be established to assist in avoiding things that may re-trigger an angry response. Identifying and communicating one's own triggers may help your partner identify and communicate their own triggers. This will make it easier to identify language and behavior to avoid.

One common and often subconscious human defense mechanism is to provoke the adversary in an attempt to make them appear to be the irrational party, thereby validating your own point of view. Agreeing to refrain from attempts to push one another's buttons serves to abbreviate the conflict.

Avoidance of critical and hurtful language is crucial if the root of the conflict is to be determined and resolved. It is easy to become involved in negative language and play the blame game. While it may make one or more of the partners feel better momentarily, it does nothing to demonstrate respect or facilitate true resolution. On the contrary, it may do long-term damage to the relationship.

Being acutely aware of one's tone of voice is also imperative to a fruitful discussion. Not only are words important, the way in which they are said is impactful. Even a phrase as simple as "I'm fine, thank you" can be interpreted several different ways depending upon its delivery. If said sweetly, it can be a gentle way to engage in conversation. If said sarcastically, it can be an accusation to make the other person feel they do not care.

Agree to continue to take strategic pauses if emotions threaten to derail the process of resolving conflict. Allow each participant in the conflict the ability to take another time out if they feel they are about to lose control.

It is human nature to be inclined to attribute all issues to the other person's character instead of limiting ill feelings to a specific behavior or contrasting view. One needs to be mindful of upholding human dignity in times of conflict. Everyone wants to be highly esteemed.

A (Actively Listen)

Authors Jack and Judith Balswick state that when families communicate in their own distinctive ways, it causes growth and a deepening of intimacy within the family. They explain if families are not talking things out, then nothing will be resolved. Instead there will be cumulative strain on the family that will have a destructive effect, benefiting no one.[1]

We agree with this viewpoint. Many times, conflict is the result of failing to truly listen to one another. Instead of listening with the intent of understanding each other's viewpoints, we sometimes listen only to respond. That is competing, *not* listening. It is quite common to spend more time formulating a response than listening to what the other person is saying. To counteract this human tendency, it is important for each party involved in a conflict to *actively* listen to each other. Listening is often considered a passive process, but we believe that listening should be active, that is, the listener is to have an active role in the listening process. What does that mean? It means demonstrating to the other person that you are indeed listening. There are a number of ways you can do this using both verbal and nonverbal language. However, when applying active listening skills, it is imperative to be sensitive to cultural differences in communication practices and to honor those as soon as you become aware of them.

Nonverbal language, commonly referred to as body language, can go a long way in making a person feel heard. For example, sitting while listening with an open and relaxed posture signals to the speaker that you are open to hearing the person's concerns, and also increases your ability to listen and maintain an open mind. Maintaining eye contact is helpful in two ways: It tells the speaker you are paying attention and also helps you to keep focused on the speaker, thereby decreasing the chances of becoming distracted during the discussion. Nodding is another nonverbal sign that serves to reinforce that you are listening and acknowledging a person's story and feelings. Keeping quiet and allowing the person to have their say for an uninterrupted time is respectful and beneficial. Allow this to happen, and try not to hurry this time. Listening is a gift that bestows respect and honor to the speaker.

Verbal language makes use of sounds, words, phrases and sentences to signify that one is listening. A person may simply say "uh-huh" or "hmm" to demonstrate tracking of the speaker's conversation. This acknowledgement helps to encourage the speaker to continue, especially since these words are neutral and do not denote agreement or disagreement. At times, the person may stop talking. They may or may not be done; they may need a breather or may be ready to find out what you are thinking. (It is important to give the speaker a bit of time to continue before beginning to respond.) At this point, the listener may feel the need to talk, and a way to do that while continuing to demonstrate that you have heard the speaker is to summarize, reflect back or ask for clarification of what the speaker has said.

A summary is a succinct paraphrase of what one has heard and understood in one's own words. Every attempt should be made to avoid using inflammatory words when summarizing, even if those have been used by the speaker. It is often more helpful to paraphrase feelings than exact words used, for example:

Speaker: You were horrible and rude and yelled at me, calling me stupid!

Listener: You felt hurt and disrespected by me when I yelled a hurtful label at you.

Clarifying is simply asking the speaker to help you understand what was meant. The listener should then summarize that part to assure the speaker that they have been heard and understood.

Reflecting back is a powerful technique. The listener will reflect back the speaker's feelings, not the story. This demonstrates to the speaker that the listener acknowledges that feelings were involved. This does not imply that the listener necessarily agrees with the speaker, but it is a powerful acknowledgement and validation of the speaker's subjective emotions, whether perceived or otherwise. As previously discussed, acknowledging another person's feelings by naming that feeling serves to calm the person even further. We have experienced this firsthand in the work we do and in our own families.

Authors Ken Sande and Tom Raabe say that when one listens, it sends an affirmative signal that the person has been heard and their views are valued. In addition, when one reflects back to the person, one is validating what they felt. They add that reflecting reduces repetition of what has already been said or the raising of voices that someone may feel they have to do in order to be heard. Reflecting back also serves to slow down the conversation, which is helpful when emotions are running high.[2]

There is much literature about the use of *I* statements instead of responding to the other person with *You* statements. We like to call them *I feel* statements. For example, instead of saying "*You* were horrible and rude…," say "*I* feel hurt and disrespected because of the harsh way you spoke to me." *You* statements put someone on the defensive. *I feel* statements evoke empathy and open up the door for a more constructive conversation.

The Chinese character "to listen" is very interesting as it seems to represent key aspects of active listening. There are five components to the character, including king, eyes, ears, the heart and undivided attention:

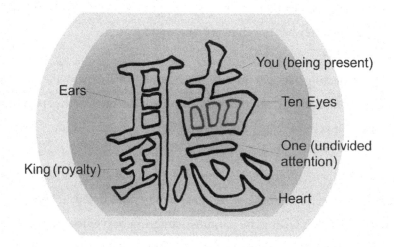

Using the key terms that comprise the symbol, listening therefore implies that one must treat the speaker like royalty, giving your undivided attention with all your senses, including your heart (empathy).[3] One should listen and observe more, and speak less. Sounds familiar, doesn't it?

When you give the speaker the honor to be heard, the likelihood of reciprocation is high. When people feel heard, respected and acknowledged, they will be ready to give the other person the same respect and acknowledgment. Active listening really is a win-win technique.

C (Choose Your Battles)

Agree to focus on the main issue at hand. If there is more than one issue, deal with each one in its own time. Conflict often involves many issues and components, particularly in a marital relationship, where several areas of irritation can build up until a full-blown conflict erupts.

For example, something as simple as an out of place shoe can be the straw that breaks the camel's back in the middle of a complex conflict. A person may label the other sloppy or irresponsible and a side conflict may erupt that has nothing to do with the main issue at hand. From there, it is downhill all the way. If a conflict is to be resolved, it is important to ensure that discussions stay on track and focused on the true source of the conflict. In other words, focus on the leaking roof causing a flood in the living room, not on the one shoe that is askew by the front door. Choose your battle: Let go of the shoe.

There are a few strategies that may be helpful in this endeavor:

1. **Let it go**: If something comes up that is not germane to the issue, then it is good to let it just slide off, like a fried egg slides off a Teflon-coated pan. The same can be said for negative statements, foul language and so forth. If the statement/action is not relevant to the issue, it is best to let it go and try to return focus to the issue at hand.

2. **Avoid the heap of dirty laundry**: Stay focused on the issue and avoid listing every little thing that has ever caused one anger. Piling issues on top of one another will overwhelm everyone and in the end, nothing tends to be resolved. Some couples dredge up past issues to further justify their reaction to the current situation. Rather, agree ahead of time to focus on the current issue and to address other conflicts one at a time, even on another day if necessary.

3. **Handle with care**: When in conflict, it is easy to focus on yourself and your own wronged feelings. This self-focus can lead to failure to consider the needs of the other person or the effects of your own behavior in the conflict. Treat others in the most equitable fashion possible. Doing this allows the discussion to remain positive and focused on resolution, not the continuation of tension and hostilities. Furthermore, it emphasizes the desire to ensure that each party feels respected and cared for, despite the current conflict.

4. **Apologize and forgive**: As alluded to earlier, sometimes a conflict cannot be resolved. In order to move on, conflicting parties will have to decide whether to make room for forgiveness despite a lack of resolution. An apology may entail apologizing for hurt inflicted or offense caused without getting into who did what. In conflict, at least one if not both parties have been hurt and offended. For an apology to truly be effective, it must contain a few components:

   · One must take responsibility for one's part in the conflict, great or small, and for actions or words that may have contributed to the conflict.

   · One must express regret for the conflict.

   · One must ask the other person what would help the other party to move forward; in other words, what will fix it?

5. **Be aware of biases**: It is important to be self-aware of common biases that influence behavior and our ability to reconcile a dispute.

Some of the biases common to humanity in general are summed up below:

- *False consensus bias*: This is the tendency to overestimate the number of people who would agree with your own opinion, values or beliefs. These are usually based on one's unscientific assumptions and may not be based on reality at all. For example, in some African cultures, being late is not a sign of disrespect, while in a more Western culture, tardiness is seen in a negative light. This disparate view of tardiness can contribute to conflict as each individual assumes their cultural view is the norm.

- *Fundamental attribution bias*: This is the tendency to ascribe someone's actions to a fundamental character flaw without recognition of external factors that may have influenced their behavior. For example, when another person is late, you may attribute that to a lack of responsibility, but when you are late, you attribute the fault to traffic conditions.

- *Recency effect*: This is the tendency to remember and place more importance on the most recent behavior than past behavior. An easy example of this is seen in the adolescent phase. A child may have been well-behaved, achieved good grades, been easy to discipline and never late for their first 15 years. When they begin dating, they occasionally return past their curfew. It is tempting for parents to focus on the recent infractions and attribute them to a character flaw, instead of remembering the pattern of good time management displayed in the past.

It is easy to become distracted with every small irritant and then lose sight of the critical issues. We encourage you to refrain from focusing on the little things and instead choose to focus on the bigger picture. A series of questions can be helpful in ascertaining the bigger picture:

- What do we all want out of this in the long term?
- What are our shared values?
- What areas can we agree on based on those values?
- Is this even worth fighting over?
- How will this conflict allow us to positively affect our future?
- Are we being too nitpicky?
- How different are our goals in this situation?

Using the above template to outline the conflict is a helpful way to stay focused on important issues and to minimize issues that are rendered irrelevant when shared values and goals are illuminated. By maintaining focus on the bigger picture, a more meaningful and lasting resolution to the conflict is possible.

E (Equip Oneself)

People often manage conflict ineffectually simply because they do not know how to manage it effectively. The good news is this is a skill that can be learned. Few people are born with the natural ability to manage conflict. We are in this line of work because we found ourselves lacking in these skills and realized we were not alone. Acquiring, utilizing and then sharing our experience is the catalyst for this book and the reason we are in the business of serving and equipping others. Today's marketplace offers many sources to equip oneself, such as seminars, workshops, podcasts, webinars. Seek these out and begin to equip yourself for your sake and the sake of your family.

Conclusion

The PEACE toolkit is just one of the countless conflict prevention, management and resolution techniques out there. We encourage you to take the time to explore the others we present, as well as those found in the work of our compatriots. With all the literature and information available, it would be profoundly sad to continue to stumble along ineffectually managing conflict when effective conflict management techniques are so accessible.

The PEACE toolkit is a helpful set of techniques for dealing with conflict. When applied consistently, these techniques can lead to a conflict resolution that is workable and respectful to both parties.

Chapter 12

The HAT Strategy

"Really, now you ask me," said Alice, very much
confused, "I don't think—"
"Then you shouldn't talk," said the Hatter.

—Lewis Carroll, *Alice in Wonderland*

Homicide Avoidance Toolkit (HAT)

This name sounds humorous, and a little over the top, but bear with us as this tool can be a relationship saver. As human beings, we all get angry at the people we are in relationship with occasionally or even daily. This tool provides a way to help you calm yourself sufficiently so you can deal with an upsetting situation in an appropriate manner.

The plain truth is, we all get angry sometimes—it is part of the human condition. While we cannot necessarily control when we get angry, we can control how we respond to anger. How we respond may serve to either harm or to heal, and the choice of response is entirely up to us.

Beyond the emotion of anger, there is a physiological response to feelings of anger. We are probably familiar with the fight, flight or freeze reflex. In the face of a strong stimulus such as fear or anger, one's instinct may be to fight back, run away or simply freeze on the spot. The feeling of anger, for example, leads to the release of adrenaline and cortisol, both of which cause accelerated blood pressure, respiration and heart rate. (Refer back to the "Amygdala Hijack" (Ch. 5) for a more thorough discussion.) The burst of energy these physiological occurrences cause often leads one to respond in an irrational manner. A rash response may serve to escalate the situation in a destructive manner. It need not be physical to be damaging. In fact, words often cause as much harm as a physical wound. Additionally, not only can anger cause damage to relationships, but if left unchecked it can lead to a myriad of medical issues, including a drastically increased risk of heart attack.

The most common advice for dealing with one's anger is to take a pause and walk away. While this is somewhat effective, it fails to adequately address the issue, particularly if you wish or are required to maintain a relationship with a person who has angered or hurt you. More often than not, you do not have the luxury of avoiding that person for the rest of your life. Whether in a personal or professional setting, it is important to learn how to get a handle on your emotions to keep a temporary emotion from causing permanent damage.

Just as there is not necessarily only one way to solve a problem, there is not one way to diffuse anger. Sometimes the simplest solution—to walk away—is all it takes. Other times it takes a run around the block, a long vent with a confidant or a journaling session to return your emotions to a manageable level. Each situation requires a different reaction and it is therefore good to know several different ways to defuse your temper.

Humor is often a good way to de-escalate tension, and that is the idea behind the tongue-in-cheek title of the Homicide Avoidance Toolkit (HAT). HAT is a compilation of various tools that are useful to manage one's anger. Let us take a closer look at what is in our HAT. It is like a magician's hat, full of easily accessible tools:

The oxygen pump: This is the simplest and easiest to describe. If at all possible, when you begin to feel as if you are going to blow your top, take a brief pause from the conversation or situation. Sometimes the pause may be as brief as a breath or two, other times you may need to count to ten, or use some deep relaxation technique to quell the desire to reach across and strangle the object of your ire. Once you have regained a modicum of composure, you may continue with the discussion.

The exit sign: Similar to the pause we discussed earlier, the exit sign is just as the name implies. It is often prudent to exit the immediate vicinity of the person or situation that has angered you. You may need to take a short walk around your cubicle or a brief respite outside. For more serious bouts of anger, it may require a longer cooling-off period.

The elliptical: Physical activity has been proven to be an effective stress reliever. Anger brings on a stress response, and exercise can help alleviate the burst of energy that often accompanies stress. This tool is useful for dealing with your own anger, and may assist the person you are in conflict with as well. Climbing on the elliptical (metaphorical or literal) yourself, or sending an upset teen on a run around the block, allows the physiological reaction to slow down, thereby returning the emotional state to a more manageable one. It is amazing to witness how expelling the burst of energy brought on by the fight, flight or freeze response can bring calm and clarity to even the angriest individual.

The Wilson (wise counselor): There was a TV show called *Home Improvement* in the 1990s. On the show, the lead character, Tim "The Toolman" Taylor, faced the normal trials of any sitcom dad of his day. He would often find himself angry and frustrated with the people in his life—both at work and home. Thankfully, Tim had a neighbor named Wilson who lived on the other side of Tim's backyard fence. When Tim needed to vent, he did not have to go any further than his own back fence. Wilson would listen with rapt attention as Tim shared his heart and expelled his frustration.

After allowing his neighbor to unburden himself, the exceedingly wise Wilson would dispense sage advice to help Tim deal with the difficult situation he found himself in. While Wilson was always sympathetic towards Tim, he wasn't afraid of speaking truth, be it encouragement or admonishment. Find your own Wilson, or even a couple of Wilsons, as they can be an invaluable tool.

The leaf blower: More often than we like to admit, our feelings of anger are unjustified. We misunderstand, we fail to listen for any other reason than to respond, we overreact and speak out of turn, we find offense when none was intended. When you find yourself in such a situation, it may be advantageous to pull out your trusty leaf blower and turn it on. In other words, let a strong wind blow away the anger and provide some fresh air to clear your head. Once the foliage of your anger has been blown away, it may become apparent that the issue is yours and yours alone.

The stud finder: Just as it is important to find a stud before hanging anything heavy on a wall, it is important to find the hidden truth of our anger's genesis before deciding how to deal with it. Is the anger a result of another's reactions? Is the anger the result of one of your buttons being pushed? Did the person who angered you have malicious intent or not? Does the anger come from a deeper, unresolved issue hiding in your psyche? The stud finder reminds you to identify what lies beneath the surface, thus helping you decide whether to confront the person who angered you or deal with the issue on your own.

The heart monitor: This tool can be used to determine the efficacy of a confrontation as well as your intent. First, determine if the issue is important enough to address. If the answer is yes, then determine if the person who has angered or hurt you will be receptive to discussing the matter. In other words, ask your heart if it will make a difference. There are different schools of thought on the benefit of confrontation; however, confrontation just for the sake of making oneself feel better can irreparably damage relationships. There are times when you need to confront a person, knowing that it will make no difference in their future actions, but that is more often an exception than a rule. In many instances, the effort and emotional toll a confrontation exacts is not worth the effort. In fact, it can lead to more anger and frustration when it becomes apparent that the assailant will not change. If you believe in your heart that confronting the individual may create a change or different outcome for yourself, others or the relationship, then it may be worth the effort. If the only change of heart you can expect is your own, your energy may be wasted, but if it leads to a change in your aggressor, then a confrontation may be warranted and constructive.

The freezer: Few things infuriate an angry person more than failing to receive an angry response in return, particularly when that person is being irrational. Remaining cool, calm and collected in the face of an aggressor's outburst can illuminate their irrationality and may serve to allow a resolution that is in our favor. This tool is exceptionally helpful in professional situations. If you can remain calm in the face of an angry co-worker, you may find yourself gaining the respect of your fellow employees and superiors.

Stationery: At times your anger is so intense that despite talking with Wilson, and using your elliptical and leaf blower, you cannot get a handle on your anger and return to rational thought. In these instances, it may be helpful to write a letter to the person who has hurt or angered you. Rarely does anyone need to read the letter; however, the act of expressing all your thoughts about the situation or person is cathartic. It is much less destructive than yelling at them or punching them in the throat. Every once in a while, you may find that the first draft is a starting point for a letter that, following much revision and time to cool off, eventually sees the light of day. Even if the letter is never sent, it can be used to assist with the dissipation of anger. As a last resort you may find it helpful to tear the letter up, put it in the bottom of your shoe and then go for a walk. With every step, you can visualize your anger being stamped out through the bottom of your shoe. Odd? Yes. Effective? Definitely.

Before we close our HAT, there is one last tool, perhaps the most important of them all, to retrieve:

Forgiveness: (Notice how often we emphasize forgiveness?) Once the confrontation is concluded, the ability to forgive is often the most difficult step, but it is also the most essential. Even if the offending party refuses to accept responsibility, for the sake of your own mental health you must find a way to forgive them and move forward, especially if it is someone you deal with frequently. Forgiveness is not dependent upon being offered an apology, but rather it is a choice you make, on your own, and with personal willingness and determination to extend grace to the other party.

To be completely clear, forgiveness does not require that you forget what happened, nor does it imply that you condone the hurtful behavior. It is prudent to take the knowledge you gained from the offense and allow it to inform future dealings with that person. Understanding how your antagonist operates makes it easier to face the next difficult situation with them in a calm, collected manner, thereby safeguarding your own health, both mental and physical.

A good habit to adopt before you confront a person who has hurt or angered you is to take some time to visit the HAT tools one by one. Select the tool you need to rationally and constructively discuss the situation. You may often find that your anger is not justified or that you are the one who needs to apologize. While there is little more humbling than the act of apologizing, the value of an apology is so often ignored.

If after using the tools, you determine that you have been truly wronged and confrontation is warranted, proceed with caution. Be sure to carry your HAT toolkit with you. No matter the outcome of the confrontation, you want to ensure that you have done everything in your power to make it as constructive an experience as possible for both yourself and the other person. Then you can walk away knowing there is nothing more you could have done to rectify the situation.

As you mature and expand your experience, you may find yourself adding tools and personalizing the HAT. You may not see the necessity of all of these tools now, but it is a good idea to hang onto them, because really, anything that can keep you out of jail is worthy of a place in your homicide avoidance toolkit!

We all get angry at times - it is part of the human condition. How we respond may serve to either harm or heal. The HAT strategy provides a way to choose our response wisely.

Chapter 13

Forgiveness

As I walked out the door toward the gate that would lead to my freedom, I knew if I didn't leave my bitterness and hatred behind, I'd still be in prison.

—Nelson Mandela

When we have been wronged, we cry out for justice. It is the human response to being hurt, maligned, abused and bullied. We expect an apology from those who have wronged us and sometimes even some type of reparation for our suffering. In a perfect world, this would happen every time and without delay. However, since we do not live in a perfect world but in one where conflict occurs every day, we are often injured by those we are in relationship with. Unresolved conflict can be catastrophic for individuals and families. An important step towards resolving conflict and reestablishing relationships is the act of forgiveness. Although the ability to forgive those who have hurt us is difficult, it is imperative if we want to live healthy lives. For this reason, we have dedicated a chapter to a discussion of forgiveness.

Of all the virtues, forgiveness feels furthest from our reach. However, within psychological circles, forgiveness is fast becoming something of a buzzword, with a growing body of scientific research indicating how transformative it can be for the injured party as well as the wrongdoer.

While the psychological benefits of forgiveness are powerful, there is increasing evidence that forgiveness is good for your physical health as well. Dr. Karen Schwartz, director of the Johns Hopkins Hospital's Mood Disorders Adult Consultation Clinic, states, "There is an enormous physical burden to being hurt and disappointed."[1] When we hold onto our hurts, we put ourselves at higher risk of major depression, heart disease, diabetes and a host of other illnesses. Conversely, there are great physical benefits from letting go of bitterness and forgiving those who have hurt us. Some of these are lowering the risk of heart attack, reducing blood pressure and pain levels, improving sleep and decreasing anxiety and depression.[2] Researchers have also studied the effect of forgiveness intervention on patients with coronary artery disease and found that when cardiac patients underwent forgiveness therapy, the blood flow to their hearts improved.[3]

Additionally, Dr. Frederic Luskin, co-founder of the Stanford Forgiveness Project at Stanford University, explains, "When you don't forgive you release all the chemicals of the stress response. Each time you react, adrenaline, cortisol and norepinephrine enter the body. When it's a chronic grudge, you could think about it 20 times a day, and those chemicals limit creativity, they limit problem-solving. Cortisol and norepinephrine cause your brain to enter what we call "the no-thinking zone," and over time, they lead you to feel helpless and like a victim. When you forgive, you wipe all of that clean."[4]

As evidence of the power of bitterness and lack of forgiveness continues to mount, it is imperative that we begin to examine what it means to forgive. We need to develop strategies to increase our ability to forgive, even when our wrongdoer is unwilling—or unable—to accept responsibility for their actions or offer an apology.

What Is Forgiveness?

Firstly, forgiveness is not about the past; it is about the future— specifically, how we choose to move forward from our hurt and slights.

Secondly, forgiveness is not about the perpetrator. It is about what is best for us, the injured party. The definition of *forgiveness* is "to give up resentment."[5] Giving up resentment does not mean excusing, it does not mean relinquishing justice and it does not require reconciliation.

Finally, it's important to understand that forgiveness does not imply you are condoning the actions of the perpetrator. By forgiving, you are not declaring that what the person did to you was correct or that it does not matter. All you are doing is letting go of the negativity associated with that event. You are saying goodbye to it and putting it in your past, ensuring you never have to expend any more energy recalling or experiencing it again. You can view it as cutting an invisible thread of resentment that continues to connect you to the perpetrator.

Some Examples of Forgiveness

Throughout human history there is an endless list of atrocities committed by the human race (or the human "disgrace"). Many of these events happened long before the expansion of our worldwide communication system. With the rise of globalization, these atrocities are on the global stage and readily visible to all.

One of the most horrific and well-known cases of injustice was that of apartheid in South Africa. The degradation and dehumanization of the majority black population was reprehensible. While there were many in South Africa and around the world who fought to end apartheid, none is more noteworthy than Nelson Mandela. Mandela was imprisoned for 27 years for his objection to apartheid, and tortured for many of those years. When he was finally released in 1990, he called for forgiveness and reconciliation. Many felt betrayed that he did not seek revenge, or at the very least, display righteous anger. The world took note. To this day, Mandela's refusal to hold on to unforgiveness and bitterness is used as an example of forgiveness in training workshops, schools and universities worldwide.

Even without the benefit of current research, Mandela understood the detrimental effect that holding onto hurts, grudges and bitterness can have on us. If a man tortured and imprisoned at the prime of his life (40 years old) for nearly three decades could find in himself forgiveness, what lessons are in that for us who get hurt, disappointed and offended in our ordinary lives? What if those who have inflicted pain on us are not even sorry for their actions? Do we only forgive those who deserve our forgiveness? If we value our own well-being, our answer to these questions must be no.

The stories of genocide survivors in Rwanda help us to understand and demonstrate that not only is forgiveness possible, but it is necessary for the health and well-being of oneself and also of the community at large:

- Jean De Dieu Musabyimana watched from a neighbor's home as the then 13-year-old's grandfather was beaten to death and his body thrown into a pit toilet. He and his mother managed to escape the initial raid on their home by hiding with neighbors, but were eventually left to fend for themselves in the jungle. Sadly, Musabyimana's mother was raped and then killed shortly after their escape as he watched from the bushes. Musabyimana credits his faith when discussing his ability to forgive those who perpetrated the genocide. He even managed to go to the home of one of the men who murdered his mother. While there he met the man's young son who asked about his mother. Musabyimana explained that she had died and the six-year-old replied, "Oh, don't worry, we are going to find her in heaven." Following his act of forgiveness, Musabyimana said he no longer felt trapped in the past, and could finally let go and move forward with his life. And now he says, "My passion is to teach the world forgiveness."[6]

- Hyppolite Ntigurirwa was seven years old when he saw his father killed and fed to dogs during the Rwandan genocide of 1994. He survived by hiding himself under dead bodies and scrounging for food in the wild and then in a refugee camp. Despite his horrific experience, Ntigurirwa found a way to forgive those who had committed the atrocities in his country, including the murder of many of his relatives. He spoke at the One Young World Summit in October of 2017 and shared his reason for forgiving the perpetrators: "I chose to forgive them, not because it is easy to forgive. It's never easy to forgive. But because I wanted them and the world to learn the price of a lasting peace. Let's make this world a better place. Let's, each one of us, be the peace."[7]

Forgiveness and Families

Just as there are no perfect people, there are no perfect families. We know that every family experiences some conflict and dysfunction. The way these dysfunctions and conflicts were managed within our family of origin has a marked effect on how we handle being wronged by others, including our capacity to forgive and move forward.

Sadly, many families are rife with not just conflict but also abuse, be it verbal, emotional, physical or any combination thereof. It is common for victims of abuse to continue to struggle later in life, thus creating difficulties when they start families of their own. Jack and Judith Balswick suggest that these individuals have unresolved feelings of helplessness and so the behavior trickles down from parent to child. These unresolved feelings lead to the formation of a family lacking in resilience. As we discussed earlier, resilience is necessary for families to recover from conflict or crisis, thus enabling them to continue to function effectively. Non-resilient families tend to focus on their troubles instead of recoverability. If there are a number of stressful events that occur in a family and members of the family do not process these events, stress can build. Upon the occurrence of the next stressful incident, an outburst of emotion often takes a family off guard.[8]

A critical component of processing stress is communication. If families are not communicating with each other, they do not share information or feelings and eventually lose the ability to cope. Communication is undoubtedly the most important attribute to have when it comes to recovering from any conflict. If there is a lack of communication, then there is no strategic planning to solve a problem or ability to set any type of achievable goal.[9] Families must be able to express themselves to one another without fear of judgment for doing so. When there is no open and honest communication within the family, then there is no working together to make necessary adjustments to prevent the conflict from happening again, or at least make it more bearable the next time conflict arises.

In families that foster open communication, it is usually easier to forgive any trespasses between family members. Often the aggressor will offer an apology, thus fostering reconciliation. Admittedly, it is much easier to forgive a person who has acknowledged their wrongdoing; however, a lack of apology in no way prevents an individual from offering forgiveness.

During the course of working through a family conflict, areas of dysfunction from our families of origin often rear their ugly heads. When this happens, it is important to address how that past bitterness may be affecting the current conflict and encourage the person holding onto that grudge to forgive their past hurts, thereby mitigating their effect on current struggles. This also prevents the cycle of family dysfunction from perpetuating itself in following generations.

Since people who forgive live happier and healthier lives, it follows that families that foster a forgiving environment experience more satisfaction and closer relationships than those that hold onto grievances.

Forgiveness Strategies

It is important to bear in mind that forgiveness isn't necessarily a feeling. It is not about forgetting or even excusing a transgression. It is about our own reaction to being hurt. In the case of someone who has offered an apology, forgiveness can be very simple and straightforward. One only needs to accept the apology and pledge to move forward from that point without bitterness or resentment. But what if no apology is offered or, in the case of many family situations, the perpetrator is no longer living? This can be more difficult, but still within reach.

Forgiving someone is a very personal and individual act. What works for one may not work for another. However, there are some fairly common ways to help you as you attempt to forgive others:

- Spend some time examining your feelings about the situation. Determining exactly why and how you have been hurt provides a framework on which to build forgiveness.
- Express your feelings about the situation. This can be done through sharing with a trusted and objective friend, therapist or even the person who has hurt you. Additionally, you can use a journal to express your feelings or write a letter to the person who hurt you. Even if you never share your feelings with your perpetrator, the act of expressing them in some tangible way can aid you in the forgiveness process.
- Put yourself in the shoes of your offender in an attempt to understand why they may have acted that way. Identifying what motivated

the person to hurt you may make it easier to forgive them, particularly if you are dealing with a long-standing family cycle of dysfunction. Understanding behavior does not minimize the extent of the damage, but it can provide a pathway to forgiveness.

- Physical expression of your feelings may also be helpful. Unexpressed anger about the situation may hinder your ability to forgive. For example, using a long walk or hard workout to release that anger before approaching forgiveness may be necessary.

- Remember that forgiveness may be a continual, lengthy process. And as you peel back the layers of your hurt, you may find other things you need to forgive your perpetrator for.

- Acknowledging that you do not have to forget in order to forgive is powerful. Rare is the instance when something cannot be learned from a situation, even one in which you were hurt. Recognizing the edifying power of hurt and experience can foster feelings of gratitude and forgiveness, which are the enemies of bitterness.

- There are an increasing number of forgiveness applications available for both computers and phones. These apps offer guided meditation to release grudges.

- Of course, when we are the perpetrators the most powerful thing we can do is offer an apology. Taking responsibility for our wrongdoing and absolving those we have hurt of any feelings of responsibility for the situation can go a long way in helping the other person process hurt and foster forgiveness.

Conclusion

At the end of the day, there are many paths to forgiveness; each individual needs to find the path that works best for them. Suffice to say, in order for a family to begin to resolve conflict and mitigate the long-term damage done, it is important for forgiveness to be a process that is incorporated into the family's value system and crisis management toolkit.

**Forgiveness is the enemy of bitterness and is
crucial to the process of family reconciliation.**

Part IV:
Let's Build!

Chapter 14

Family Resilience

"She stood in the storm, and when the wind did not
blow her way, she adjusted her sails."

—Elizabeth Edwards

We believe the best way to close out this book is to discuss prevention.
Thus far, we have spent much time discussing various skills and tools to
use in the successful management of conflict. Let us now turn to another
topic we are passionate about: resilience. Families that are resilient will
withstand the inevitable winds of conflict.

What Is Resilience?

Did you ever beg your parents for a quarter to buy a bouncy ball
out of a turnstile vending machine? When your parents gave in to your
request, you took that quarter, placed it in the red machine and anxiously
awaited that brightly colored ball of joy. Throw after throw, those balls
never failed to bounce. No matter the amount of force, direction or obstacle, they bounced back. It was a rite of passage for many children, particularly American children. In addition to providing hours of entertainment,
for many of us a bouncy ball provided our first tangible experience with
resilience. As humans, we all have the potential to be resilient—just like
those 25-cent rainbow-colored balls of joy. Sometimes we just need some
guidance.

There are many definitions of *resilience*. The American Psychological Association defines resilience as "the process of adapting well in the face of adversity, trauma, tragedy, threats or significant sources of stress—such as family and relationship problems, serious health problems, or workplace and financial stressors... resilience involves 'bouncing back' from these difficult experiences."[1] Resilience is also described as the "positive or adaptive outcome during a stressful situation in daily life challenges and/or trauma."[2] According to *Merriam-Webster Online*, resilience is "an ability to recover from or adjust easily to misfortune or change."[3] When it comes to family resilience, Froma Walsh defines it as "the ability of the family, as a functional system, to withstand and rebound from adversity."[4]

Drawing from these definitions, we have formulated our own definition of family resilience: the ability to get through a traumatic, hurtful or life-changing event in a way that results in family relationships remaining intact, individuals remaining functional and the family unit recovering from the crisis.

How Is Family Resilience Challenged?

As individuals, we all have differing levels of resilience. Some of us are hardwired to be resilient, while others are lacking in natural resilience. Additionally, the strategies employed to activate resilience in the face of adversity vary from person to person. There is no "right way" to be resilient. Thankfully, whether a person is naturally resilient or not does not preclude them from becoming resilient, as resilience can be learned. Conversely, even if one is naturally resilient, failure to employ resilient characteristics on a regular basis can lead to a decreased capacity for resilience. Just as muscles we fail to use on a regular basis atrophy, resilience can diminish if not utilized regularly.

Due to its collaborative nature, family resilience is not just an individual endeavor. While family members each have their own level of proficiency employing resilience, the family as a whole has its own measure of resilience. Determining the resilience of a family unit by pointing out their history of overcoming adversity can be helpful in successfully resolving conflict within that family.

Anytime a family faces a difficulty—be it physical, financial, emotional—stress rears its ugly head. Even happy occasions like the birth of a new child or a wedding come with both heightened emotions and feelings of stress. Additionally, events that a family believes they have prepared for, such as graduations and retirement, may still cause a significant amount of stress. Stress challenges even the most resilient families.

How a family deals with stressors is a good indicator of their resilience. Families that choose to avoid dealing with stress as it occurs, thus stockpiling their stress, risk dealing with a larger outburst of emotion than they may be able to quickly mitigate when a future stressful event occurs. However, families that routinely deal with stress as it arises (and prepare in advance for upcoming stressful events) tend to experience less disruption and/or negative consequences related to those events. In short, resilient families experience less conflict as a result of stress than non-resilient families do.

How Is Family Resilience Achieved?

Just as there are many different definitions of resilience, there are a multitude of theories on how resilience is expressed in families and what the key factors in building resilience actually are. We will examine a few of those we found most helpful in our pursuit of understanding and fostering family resilience in our own families.

The Work of Froma Walsh

Froma Walsh is a therapist who has dedicated her career to the field of resilience. Walsh outlines characteristics promoting resilience in a family. We have selected four key characteristics that encapsulate the crux of her resilience work:[5]

1. Making meaning of adversity: This means normalizing or contextualizing the stress a family may go through. We believe making meaning is fundamental to who we are as human beings. It can also be helpful to have a shared belief system to cope with events that impact the family in a negative way.

2. A positive outlook: The family that has hope will be better able to cope. Positivity lends itself to hope, which is a fundamental attribute that causes family members to encourage one another, affirm their strengths and promote a can-do spirit. Furthermore, the family will be able to master what is possible and accept the reality that some things cannot be changed.

3. **Transcendence and spirituality**: Families that use this coping technique have a higher sense of value and purpose that drives them to overcome adversities. They are creative, and willing to learn and change—characteristics that will result in positive growth.

4. **Open emotional sharing**: This coping technique includes sharing of deep emotions and/or deep pain such as sorrow or suffering. Even anger and fear should be shared openly and honestly. Positive emotions also need to be shared, such as appreciation, humor, joy or relief in the midst of the stressful event. Sharing not only helps to process and make meaning of adversities, but also helps to unify the family—they are in this together.

The Work of Jack and Judith Balswick

Jack Balswick is a family sociologist and Judith Balswick is a licensed marriage and family therapist. The couple teaches, researches and helps families be more effective in their relationships. They suggest that in order for families to overcome adversities, they must learn how to cope with or withstand life challenges. Life stressors are observed in three different interactions with a stressful event: 1) how the family manages the actual event that caused the stress, 2) resources the family has access to at the time the event occurs and 3) how the family perceives the event.[6]

They further explain that if there are a number of stressful events that occur in a family and members of the family either do not want to deal with it, or do not know how, stress will likely build up. Consequently, conflict will be very likely. They suggest five problem-solving stages that have resonated with us and our own family experience:[7]

1. Acknowledge there is a problem that needs to be dealt with.
2. Make a conscious decision to resolve the problem and not engage in defensive avoidance as this will prohibit a constructive approach to the resolution of the problem.
3. Gather information that will help effectively solve the problem and decide which option will best work to resolve it.
4. Evaluate the selected option and determine if it should be utilized, revised or completely disregarded for a different strategy.
5. Determine if the problem has been resolved. If not, the family should start the process over again until a workable solution is found.

The Work of the American Psychological Association

The American Psychological Association offers several factors that contribute to the building of resilience. These include:[8]

- Having caring and supportive relationships within and outside the family.
- The capacity to make realistic plans and take steps to carry them out.
- A positive view of yourself and confidence in your strengths and abilities.
- Communication and problem-solving skills.
- The capacity to manage strong feelings and impulses.

Notice how the various works discussed thus far share common themes.

The Work of Dorothy Becvar

Dorothy Becvar is a licensed clinical social worker and licensed marital and family therapist with decades of experience on family resilience. Becvar's focus is on three domains in which families should be resilient:[9]

1. **Belief systems:** Such systems include finding meaning in life, normalizing issues, having a positive outlook, thoroughly appraising a cause and developing a relational view of family strength and spirituality.
2. **Organizational patterns:** The family's organizational structure should be flexible enough to adapt to change while retaining connectedness and making effective use of available resources.
3. **Communication/problem-solving:** Clear and consistent communication, resourcefulness, humor, emotional expression, conflict repair, focus on goals and proactively planning are valuable skills and expressions that can be learned and adopted.

Becvar also views family resilience as a progression broken down into five phases outlined below.[10] We have found these phases invaluable when facing challenging life events as they provide a hopeful progression toward healing:

Phase 1: Survival: In this phase the stressful event has recently occurred and the family is using the most basic survival skills to cope.

Phase 2: Adaptation: The family has surfaced from trying to survive the shock and reality of the stressful event and is now navigating the change the event has brought. The family will need to espouse the "new normal" of reality in the aftermath of the crisis and make some adjustments and accommodations to realign with this new reality.

Phase 3: Acceptance: Once the family has successfully adjusted to the stressful event by making necessary changes and accommodations, it will be ready and able to make peace with the occurrence of the stressful event. It is at this point that we believe a visible recovery will be evident in the life of the family.

Phase 4: Growing Stronger: After achieving recovery, the family unit is able to rebuild its strength. It is in this phase that resilience is "at home" in the family unit. In other words, resilience is not just developing—it is being experienced by each family member. Growing stronger happens exponentially from this stage onward.

Phase 5: Helping Others: This phase is best described as moving from "surviving to thriving." When a family has moved from a place of barely keeping its head above water into a place of being able to throw a lifeline to other families in crisis, they have demonstrated the ultimate level of resilience. The desire to help others is a key factor in building and fostering resilient communities.

Attributes of a Resilient Family

Informed by the above discussions, we believe the following factors are key to building and expressing family resilience:

- Sharing a belief system that acknowledges crisis as a difficult and/or unexpected life event that, albeit traumatic, is a normal part of life.
- Willingness to work together to navigate crises.
- Agreement to reach out to available resources for assistance.
- A positive outlook that fosters hope of resolve, recovery and rebuilding.
- An altruistic approach where family members can visualize eventually being able to help others recover from similar life events.

Conclusion

Resilience is a shortcut to conflict resolution. If you are dealing with a family made up of resilient people, resolving conflicts is much easier than in families with little resiliency. Families lacking in resilience often have more conflict and increased difficulty in resolving conflict. Thankfully, resilience is (while naturally easier for some) a skill set that can be learned and employed no matter one's age or situation. It behooves those of us who desire to decrease conflict within our own families, and assist other families as they navigate conflict, to hone our own resilience, thus becoming role models to others.

Resilience is one of the leading indicators of how easily conflict can be resolved within a family and how damaging failure to resolve conflict can be to a family. Although it is easier for some people to be more resilient than others, this skill set can be learned by everyone.

Chapter 15

Building a Resilient House

It is not the beauty of a building you should look at; it's the construction of the foundation that will stand the test of time.

—David Allan Coe

Family Formation

Earlier we discussed the definition of *family*. We described how families differ greatly in their makeup but have some key similarities. Building a family is much like building a house. And just like families can look different from the outside, so can the houses they live in. There is wide variance in the numbers of rooms, building materials, furnishings, and decorating styles. However, there are still some basic structures found in all homes, just as there are some basic structures found in healthy families. For the purposes of illustrating some of these basic structures and finding areas that either have already produced conflict within a family—or have the potential to—we use the analogy of building a physical house. We will use this analogy to examine a few key structures that are found in homes, namely, the foundation, the kitchen, the living room, the bedroom, the bathroom and the garage.

The Foundation

The most important factor in a stable home is a solid foundation. Without that, the entire house will collapse. There are some crucial building blocks that need to be in place in order to form a strong family foundation. Ideally a family begins with its foundation in place, but that is not always the case. Additionally, families may experience conflict as a result of shifts or changes in the foundation of their home.

We have identified three components found in stable family foundations, no matter the size or makeup of a family:

- Love and commitment
- Shared values and purpose
- Team orientation

Let us take a deeper dive into each of these fundamentals and then explore how they may challenge the integrity of the foundation in times of crisis:

Love and Commitment

Most families begin when two adults who love each other make a commitment to live life together. This commitment merges two individual lives into a new shared, familial life. As a family expands to include children, the commitment extends to the next generation.

It is a common misconception that love is a feeling. While it definitely includes an emotional component, love is more than that. It is also a decision to put the needs of another on the same level as—or higher—than your own. Anyone who has been married for a while can attest to the fact that there are days that you just don't "feel the love." On those days, love is a choice to continue in the relationship despite not experiencing the feelings of love.

Love is also a choice to care for another in the good times and the bad. Love is why a husband brings his wife flowers on a random Tuesday. Love is what motivates a person to get up and tend to an ailing spouse or child in the middle of the night. Love is why a parent goes to work every day to provide for the family, even when they do not feel like it. It is why a mother cries with her heartbroken child. All of these actions are the product of a choice to love another person.

Commitment is the decision to continue in a relationship. It is the resolution to stay attached to another person and an agreement to function as part of a larger system. Commitment is not always easy, particularly during times of waning passion. However, persevering and honoring one's commitment is a crucial aspect in the foundation of a family.

Furthermore, commitment may be a matter of legality when two individuals marry. A marriage certificate issued by a government institution is a legal contract between two people that signifies their agreement to intertwine their lives. When one or both parties decide to abandon their commitment through divorce, it requires the involvement of the courts as well as the family members.

Shared Values and Purpose

We believe the strongest foundation of a family is formed when the members of the family share the same values and purpose. These values can include all manner of subjects ranging from religious beliefs, economic desires and the importance of expanding the family to the type of home the family wants to live in. When the values of any member of the family skew too far from the standard, there is conflict.

The purpose of a family is also important. Just as values differ greatly from family to family, so does purpose. Some families view their purpose as merely a vehicle for procreation, others as a force for good in the world. Still others view family as an economic advantage.

No matter the purpose of any given family, it is important for the stability of a family to share values and purpose. Without agreement on that, a home can quickly find itself in danger of collapse.

Team Orientation

When two people commit to one another, it is implied that they move from a self-centered identity to a shared one. In essence, they form a team. The beauty of a team mentality is the recognition that each family member has their own set of strengths and weaknesses. Ideally, these strengths and weaknesses are complementary and allow a family to be stronger together than each of its individuals on their own.

Once the foundation of a family has been laid, it is time to begin working on the rooms in the house. While every family is different, there are some rooms that are common to most families. Each of these rooms is typically also connected to one of the foundational building blocks. In the following section, we will examine some of the typical rooms found in a family's home and then identify some ways in which the foundation under those rooms may be compromised during a family crisis.

A Closer Look at Each Room

1. **The Kitchen:** The kitchen is typically the most functional of all the rooms in a house. It is where the physical need for sustenance of a family is met, and is often where much of the family business is conducted, be it bill paying or homework completion. Just as every

family is different, so is the kitchen in every home. Some kitchens are elaborate with restaurant grade appliances, while others are simple and basic with only the bare essentials. Our metaphorical kitchen contains some basic information about a family:

· Who is employed and what they do for work
· Distribution of labor within the home
· Financial needs/goals
· Physical needs

A well-functioning kitchen is imperative. When families agree upon the basics like finances and distribution of labor, there is harmony. If this room is lacking in the basic necessities, a family's capacity to care for itself is compromised and meeting needs becomes a real challenge. The kitchen typically straddles both the "Shared Values and Purpose" and the "Team Orientation" segments of the family's foundation.

Unfortunately, since the kitchen is the financial hub of the home, it is particularly susceptible to cracks and fissures. Financial stress is often cited by divorcing couples as a major source of stress in their marriage, particularly when there is little to no agreement on how finances are managed and utilized.[1] Disagreements about the distribution of labor (both within and outside of the household) are also common. When one partner feels as if they are carrying more of the load than the other, financially, emotionally or physically, the entire household suffers. Furthermore, when a family is struggling to keep a roof over its head and everyone's bellies full, the probability of serious conflict increases.

2. **The Living Room:** Most homes have at least one common lounging room, typically that is the living room. While this space is one in which the entire family congregates, it is also the part of the home that is on display when company comes over. It is both a public

and private space, and therefore represents both the private and public persona of the family. The living room functions as the place where:

- The family spends time together.
- The family shares their emotions.
- The family has fun together.
- The family entertains friends and relatives (it serves as the public face of the family).

The living room is often the emotional center of the home as well as the entertainment center. In this room families share their feelings, talk and laugh together. It is often the place where the family spends time snuggled together on the couch enjoying a movie, playing board games or simply sitting together at the end of each day. People who love one another typically want to spend time together and foster intimacy through the sharing of their lives. As such, these activities are built upon the "Love and Commitment" section of the family's foundation.

Fissures in this part of the family tend to be emotional in nature. Emotions are powerful and when expressed in an unhealthy manner can be disastrous to a family, most notably during arguments when one or more family members experiences an amygdala hijack. Also, as the place where the family spends time together, the living room is often where families become annoyed by each other's habits.

It is easy to let a bunch of small annoyances and/or disagreements pile up until their combined weight cracks the foundation. Pride very often plays a part in family discord and must be dealt with carefully. Confrontation may also lead to one or more family members becoming defensive. The ability of family members to act with humility, and their willingness to apologize and learn from the situation, is indicative of the type of outcome the family will experience.

As the living room is also the space most frequently opened to visitors, the public persona of the family resides here. This room is often a source of pride displaying the best the family has to offer in the way of behavior and furnishings. It can be an outward representation of the socioeconomic status of the family.

Finally, since the living room represents the public face of the family, this common space also relies on the "Team Orientation" section of the foundation. Families that are working well as a team present a united front to the world. Those in conflict often take their dissatisfaction outside of the home with them. This can affect things like their performance at school or work and relationships with friends and extended family.

3. **The Bedroom:** The bedroom is the only truly private room in a home. It is also the place where couples share intimacy, both physically and emotionally, and the space to which each member can retreat when they need time alone.

   Each member of the family may or may not have their own room. While the function of the furniture in this room slightly differs for children and their parents, a bedroom is the place of respite and retreat.

   The main purposes of our metaphorical bedroom are:
   · Fostering and maintaining intimacy.
   · Individual downtime and solitude.

   The metaphorical bedroom is invaluable when it comes to times of conflict, particularly when one needs to take a strategic pause. The bedroom represents a quiet place to decompress and calm down. Each member of the family can retreat to their own space with their own thoughts and take the time they need to prepare to deal with the conflict in a productive manner.

The marital bedroom forms a secondary foundation for the children. When a married couple experiences harmony and both partners are satisfied with their level of intimacy, it sets the tone for the rest of the household.

For a family's offspring, a bedroom's main purpose is to provide a private space—a place where they can spend time dealing with their own thoughts and feelings—and, in times of conflict, a place of respite.

The "Love and Commitment" section of a family's foundation is usually where the bedrooms are found. For a married couple, the bedroom is the place they connect intimately, and in times of stress it is often the first connection to suffer. If one or both members of the couple feel as if their needs—emotional and/or physical—are not being met, there can be conflict. Feelings of being taken for granted are common among couples. Differences in desire for sex can lead to conflict and may be a factor in the seeking out of extramarital affairs to satisfy unmet needs. Additionally, differing expectations related to sex, finances, chore sharing and so forth can disrupt the harmony of the couple's bedroom and, if not effectively tended to, the entire household.

4. **The Bathroom:** No home is truly complete without a bathroom. It is a place of cleansing, both physically and metaphorically. There is no other room in the house where you can be as free to be your bare self.

5. **The Garage:** Perhaps no room in a home is more versatile than a garage, which functions in very different ways depending upon the family living in the house. In some homes, the garage is a space to house a vehicle. In other homes, it is a storage space. In others, it

can be another entertainment space. Some of the things you may find in a garage are:

· The family vehicle.
· Tools for the completion of maintenance.
· Boxes/baggage (empty or full).
· Projects (completed or otherwise).

The family's working vehicle is analogous to the family's trajectory in life, with its goal being to move forward. It is easy to get stuck in the mud of the pitfalls of life, but with the right equipment, like a four-wheel drive truck, or good communication skills and the ability to work as a team, a family can navigate dangerous terrain together. A well-maintained set of relational skills keeps the vehicle tuned up and road ready. A breakdown in any area of life can cause difficulties in a family's motivation to continue its journey.

Tools are commonly found in the garage. In our metaphorical home, these tools would be how the family relates to one another, how they handle stresses and how they maintain the function of their familial relations. Good communication skills, active listening, conflict resolution skills, humility and the ability to apologize and offer forgiveness are all tools that are essential to a healthy family. If these tools are lacking or have been neglected for too long, the family will be more susceptible to stress and conflict.

The garage can be fraught with all sorts of dangers and warning signs. It is a convenient place to hide things, like the unpacked baggage from long-ago relationships, events and/or misunderstandings. Illumination of these issues is key to resolving them and keeping them from causing fissures in the foundation of a family. Often, when facing conflict, it may become apparent that the current source of conflict is merely an indication of a larger, underlying issue that has been stuffed away in the garage.

Finally, it is common to find projects in the garage. Completed projects are representative of a family's resilience and a testament to their commitment. They demonstrate the ability to work together to accomplish a goal and the existence of motivation to continue on in their shared life. Unfortunately, unfinished projects can be perilous. We notice current American society may view many things in life as disposable, things like commitment, relationships and even marriages. Unfinished projects in a family's garage may be symbolic of issues with feelings of disposability and unwillingness to stay committed. If those things are left undisturbed and unresolved, a family may be doomed to destruction.

Families with a well-organized and functioning garage tend to deal with the stresses of life in a healthy manner. They face an obstacle together, work through the necessary emotions or tasks and come out stronger on the other side. Families that lack the ability to do that can become mired in conflict.

Being that the garage is so versatile, its placement on the familial foundation varies from family to family and may even shift during the course of a family's lifetime. Struggles with the "Love and Commitment" section of the foundation are evidenced by unfinished projects. The "Shared Values and Purpose" may be eroded by differing desires for the family's trajectory and goals in life, for example, where they are taking their vehicle. "Team Orientation" fissures may show up as the avoidance of issues and the inability or unwillingness of family members to openly communicate or deal with issues lurking in the dark corners and dusty boxes.

Throughout this book we have presented many tools and techniques to deal with and resolve family conflict. In this chapter we discussed the basic building blocks of a healthy, resilient family and identified foundational areas that can create conflict. Now that we have identified these things and equipped ourselves with several tools, it is time to put it all into action. What can we do to keep a family from collapsing and/or create a stronger, more resilient family? Just as we would with a physical house, we renovate!

Before renovations can begin it is important to have a blueprint. To assist in the drafting of one, we have developed a tool called the FEEM Matrix.

The FEEM Matrix

Even with the strongest of foundations, every family will face crises. During these critical periods of a family's life, it is important to be able to work through the crisis. Failure to do so can lead to an unsatisfactory home life and may eventually lead to the total dissolution of the family.

Families, clinicians and mediators who are dealing with a family in crisis can employ our FEEM Matrix to identify the fissures in a family, determine the cause of fissures and provide a pathway to resolution of the crisis.

The FEEM Matrix provides a framework to examine the issue from all aspects in which it affects the family structure by addressing four key components, namely, foundation, expectation, education and motivation. A series of questions specific to each area can provide insight into which components of the family structure are involved in a crisis:

1. F (Foundation):

- Is the family struggling in any of the areas that form their foundation?
- Is there a lack of love and/or commitment?
- Is there a lack of agreement on values and/or purpose?

- Are there family members still committed to each other or have they placed their own desires ahead of what is best for the entire team?

2. E (Expectation):

- Does each member of the family have realistic expectations for the other members?
- Have they set the bar too high?
- Have members clearly communicated their expectations to the other family members?
- Have expectations changed on the part of one or more family members, and if so, have these expectations been communicated?

3. E (Education):

- Is the family equipped in ways to manage conflict?
- Is it a lack of knowledge of communication skills that have contributed to the breakdown?
- Are the members willing to spend time learning skills to mitigate conflict?
- What type of educational resources does the family have access to?

4. M (Motivation):

- How motivated is the family to continue living in the house they have built?
- Is there a disparate amount of motivation between partners/ members?
- Have the motivations for forming the family changed over time?
- Are members willing to realign their motivations?

Utilizing the FEEM Matrix is helpful in formulating a plan to reconcile conflict and identify ways to build a stronger, more resilient family. In combination with conflict management tools, the matrix also assists in forming a plan of action to either help a family begin (or return to) healthy functioning. Furthermore, it can encourage healthy families to be alert to possible impending conflict and address it before it gains a foothold.

Conclusion

Ideally, families begin on a strong foundation and build from there. Unfortunately, many families either start on less than solid ground or face storms in life that erode their foundations. These disruptions often cause conflict. Determining the underlying issues involved in the conflict helps families resolve their conflict and increases satisfaction within family life. Even the healthiest of families can benefit from the occasional checkup or, to use our house illustration, a little renovation. Understanding common issues families face and the FEEM Matrix are invaluable tools in the pursuit of healing, rebuilding and shoring up the foundation of healthy families.

Resilient families understand that a firm family foundation is imperative to maintaining a healthy family and weathering conflict, as is working together to build a strong house.

Part V:
Final Thoughts

Chapter 16

Intervention and Referrals

We don't have to do all of it alone. We were never
meant to.

—Brené Brown

We have analyzed family conflict by looking at the anatomy of a family,
its structure and life cycle, as well as a number of tools and techniques to
manage family conflict. We have also discussed the power of forgiveness
and characteristics needed to build family resilience. It is important to
underscore that one's own family conflicts are, and will be, some of the
most difficult conflicts to resolve. It is much easier to work with other
people's families than with your own. Furthermore, it is important to
remember that not all conflicts, be they in your family or in a family you
are working with, will be resolved.

By applying the principles outlined in the preceding chapters, you
will have displayed an intention to TRY and encourage families to resolve
issues and manage their own conflicts. The acronym *TRY* stands for:

T (Time): Plan a time for conflicting parties to come together to
talk. *Use your tools.*

R (Reason together): Spend some time discussing the issues and
listening to one another's perspectives. *Use your tools.*

Y (Yes): The ultimate goal is to guide conflicting parties to Yes—an
agreement, a resolution and/or understanding. *Use your tools.*

So, what happens when strategies, tools and techniques have been applied but have not achieved the desired outcome of resolution or peace? Do not despair! Instead, develop a referral plan. Never leave a family hanging, whether it is yours or someone else's. Plan the next course of action and refer them to further professional assistance.

While you may not feel like an expert at the moment, you should at least be a confident "first responder." In other words, you may be able to save a life (the breakup of a relationship or family) by applying the tools you have acquired to prevent a conflict from escalating to the point of no return. You may be able to prevent fatalities, just like a person administering first aid.

For more complex conflicts, you may need to refer a family—or even your family—to an expert in the field of conflict management, just like a person administering first aid may need to refer the patient to a physician for further intervention. Consider family relationships like the human body, a natural system. Consider conflict in the family (the body) as inevitable as a common cold. A person administering first aid should have a basic understanding of the anatomy of the family as well as an understanding of conflict specific to families. A first responder should also know what is in the first aid kit: the tools needed for first aid. This is exactly the journey you have taken in this book.

So how does one go about preparing an intervention and referral strategy? In the field of dispute resolution, there are a variety of mechanisms such as mediation, conflict coaching, facilitation, among others, that may be utilized to help families in complex and chronic disputes. Families may also be referred to therapists, medical practitioners, lawyers and educators to assist the family in more specialized areas of need.

Conflicts may have multiple layers of issues. Some may be perfect for mediation, such as probate matters in which a will is in dispute. Other conflicts may have issues with a need for therapeutic intervention better suited for counseling, such as learning communication skills in a relationship. Some conflicts may need medical intervention, such as where one spouse is entering a state of dementia and the other spouse thinks there is a relationship problem. A suitable intervention or referral strategy may not always be apparent from the onset. However, you need to be prepared to formulate a referral plan if it becomes necessary.

Whether it is a personal conflict or a conflict involving multiple people, it is important to be cognizant of the different options available in your area, especially if you work with families in conflict. Once you have researched these resources, reach out and introduce yourself to those you feel may be a viable referral option. Let them know the work you do and indicate your desire to consider including them in the formulation of a referral plan for families that need more than you are equipped to handle. Most providers will be happy to work with you. Do not hesitate to outsource, especially when you have already applied the tools you have learned and need further help. If in doubt, refer out.

The table below is an example of a working document you could tailor-make for yourself and keep handy. We suggest you find two to three referral options to give out. This ensures families have the autonomy to research those options for themselves, look for a good fit and make their own selection.

Professional	Area of Expertise	Contact Details
Mediators	E.g., Probate, Divorce Agreements, Real Estate	
Conflict Coaches	E.g., Couples, Individuals, Adolescents	
Counselors	E.g., Marriage & Family, Substance Abuse, Children & Parenting	
Healthcare Providers	E.g., Primary Care Practitioner, Psychiatrist, Pediatrician	
Lawyers	E.g., Family, Criminal, Probate Law	
Other	Family Crisis Centers, Courts, Centers of Urgent Intervention	

Working with families, especially your own, is difficult. In our desire to help others, one may be tempted to continue working on an issue even when it is beyond our ability to do so. We do not like to leave things undone. Instead of viewing the act of referring out as a personal failure, consider it as employing wisdom. The wise are aware of their own skill level and limitations, and are not afraid to outsource if it is in the best interest of others.

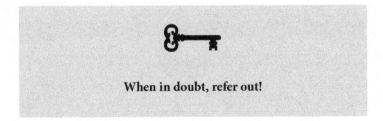

When in doubt, refer out!

Chapter 17

Conclusion

What counts in life is not the mere fact that we have lived. It is what difference we have made to the lives of others that will determine the significance of the life we lead.

—Nelson Mandela

Throughout these chapters, we have determined that family is difficult to define and often elicits very strong emotions, one way or another. One thing that binds us universally is that we all originate from a family, traditional or not. Additionally, whether positively or negatively, we have all been impacted by our families of origin.

We also bring some part of our familial experience into our adulthood. At the moment of self-awareness, we have to decide whether to continue the positive impact or turn any negative impact from that experience into opportunity. Irrespective of our age of awareness, it is never too late to make choices that will change the trajectory of our hearts. What may have started as a difficult journey in life may turn into resilience in adulthood.

Choices can be made throughout your life to turn adversity, mistakes, weaknesses and traumas into powerful opportunities for growth. Growth is achieved when you recognize the elements on your path that are not fulfilling, accept that you deserve to be fulfilled and make choices to move closer to fulfillment.

Our hope is that you have found enough keys through these chapters to unlock some of your treasure troves, and that the treasures therein may be unlocked in your lives. May you find healing, reconciliation, forgiveness, resilience and peace.

While on that path, you will know when you are ready to help others get there too. The importance of a healthy family unit for the optimal functioning of society at large cannot be emphasized enough. The more well-functioning families in the world, the better the health of society in general. Once we begin to nurture our own family into a well-functioning unit, we will be able to help others do the same. This is a great and noble endeavor.

Treasure your family, forgive those who caused you pain, let go of the past and embrace an exciting future of release and fulfillment. It is possible and it is never too late to start!

—Angela and Shannon

References (by chapter)

Chapter 1

1. *Merriam-Webster OnLine*, s.v. "family," accessed March 13, 2018, https://www.merriam-webster.com/dictionary/family.
2. *Merriam-Webster OnLine*, s.v. "nuclear family," accessed March 13, 2018, https://www.merriam-webster.com/dictionary/nuclear%20family.
3. Ibid., s.v. "family."
4. Courtney G. Joslin, "The Evolution of the American Family," *American Bar Association Human Rights Magazine* 36, no. 3 (July 1, 2009), https://www.americanbar.org/groups/crsj/publications/human_rights_magazine_home/human_rights_vol36_2009/summer2009/the_evolution_of_the_american_family.
5. US Census Bureau, "Subject Definitions," accessed August 30, 2017, https://www.census.gov/programs-surveys/cps/technical-documentation/subject-definitions.html#family.
6. Lynda Laughlin," Who's Minding the Kids? Child Care Arrangements: Spring 2011," *Household Economic Studies* (April 2013), accessed August 30, 2017, https://www2.census.gov/library/publications/2013/demo/p70-135.pdf.
7. *Merriam-Webster OnLine*, s.v. "family."

Chapter 2

1. Nichols, M.P., *Family Therapy: Concepts and Methods (11thEd.).* (New Jersey: Pearson Education Ind., 2017), 4.
2. "Person-Centered Therapy (Rogerian Therapy)," *GoodTherapy.org* (blog), January 17, 2018, www.goodtherapy.org/learn-about-therapy/types/person-centered.
3. "Adlerian Psychology/Psychotherapy," *GoodTherapy.org* (blog), October 4, 2016, www.goodtherapy.org/learn-about-therapy/types/adlerian-psychology.
4. Murray Bowen, *Family Therapy in Clinical Practice* (Lanham, MD: Rowan & Littlefield Publishers, 1985).

5. Ibid.
6. Ibid.
7. Herbert Goldenberg and Irene Goldenberg, *Family Therapy: An Overview* (Belmont, CA: Brooks/Cole, 2013).
8. William Glasser, *Choice Theory: A New Psychology of Personal Freedom* (New York: HarperCollins, 1998).
9. Ibid.
10. Ibid.

Chapter 3

1. Daniel J. Siegel, *Brainstorm: The Power and Purpose of the Teenage Brain* (New York: Penguin Group, 2013).
2. *Merriam-Webster OnLine*, s.v. "boomerang child," accessed April 3, 2020, https://www.merriam-webster.com/dictionary/boomerang%20child.
3. *Merriam-Webster OnLine*, s.v. "sandwich generation," accessed April 3, 2020, https://www.merriam-webster.com/dictionary/sandwich%20 generation.
4. Kids Count Data Center, "Single Parents Are Raising More Than One-Third of U.S. Kids" (June 12, 2018), https://datacenter.kidscount.org/updates/ show/204-single-parents-are-raising-more-than-one-third-of-us-kids.
5. Emily Badger, "The Relationship Between Single Mothers and Poverty is Not as Simple as it Seems," *The Washington Post* (April 10, 2014), https:// www.washingtonpost.com/news/wonk/wp/2014/04/10/the-relationship-between-single-mothers-and-poverty-is-not-as-simple-as-it-seems/.

Chapter 4

1. John Ng, *Dim Sum for the Family: Tips for Couples and Parents* (Singapore: Armour Publishing 2009, p. 222).
2. Ibid., 216, 219.
3. Jack Balswick and Judith Balswick, *The Family: A Christian Perspective on the Contemporary Home* (Grand Rapids, MI: Baker Publishing, 2014).
4. Craig E. Runde and Tim A. Flanagan, *Becoming a Conflict Competent Leader: How You and Your Organization Can Manage Conflict Effectively* (San Francisco: Jossey-Bass, 2012

5. Ken Sande and Tom Raabe, *Peacemaking for Families: A Biblical Guide to Managing Conflict in Your Home* (Carol Stream, IL: Tyndale House, 2002).

6. Speed B. Leas, *Moving Your Church Through Conflict* (Trinity Church, NY: Alban Institute, 1985).

Chapter 5

1. Daniel Goleman, *Emotional Intelligence: Why It Can Matter More Than IQ* (New York: Bantam Dell, 2006).

2. Daniel J. Siegel, "Brain Insights and Well-Being," *drdansiegel.com* (blog), January 22, 2015, https://www.drdansiegel.com/blog/2015/01/22/brain-insights-and-well-being-3/.

Chapter 6

1. NIH/National Institute of Mental Health, "Imaging Study Shows Brain Maturing," *ScienceDaily* (May 18, 2004), www.sciencedaily.com/releases/2004/05/040518074211.htm.

2. Ibid.

3. Ibid.

4. Daniel J. Siegel, *Brainstorm: The Power and Purpose of the Teenage Brain* (Vancouver: Langara College, 2013).

5. Ibid.

6. Ibid.

7. Ibid.

Chapter 7

1. Paul K. Chafetz, *Loving Hard-to-Love Parents: A Handbook for Adult Children of Difficult Older Parents* (Dallas: Metro Graphics, 2017).

2. Ibid., ix.

3. Richard K. Caputo, ed., *Challenges of Aging on U.S. Families: Policy and Practice Implications* (Haworth, NY: Haworth Press, 2005), 1.

4. Ibid., 9.

5. Ibid., 10.

6. Ibid., 12.

7. Ibid., 14.

8. Ibid., 15

9. John M. Campanola, "The Sandwich Generation is Growing, and So Are Their Responsibilities," *Delray Newspaper* (March 2017), http://delraynewspaper.com/sandwich-generation-growing-responsibilities-23626

10. Ibid.

11. National Institute on Aging, *Participating in Activities You Enjoy* (2015), https://www.nia.nih.gov/health/publication/participating-activities-you-enjoy.

Chapter 9

1. William Glasser, *Choice Theory: A New Psychology of Personal Freedom* (New York: HarperCollins, 1998).

2. *Quotes.net*, s.v. "Elie Wiesel," accessed February 16, 2019, https://www.quotes.net/quote/18973.

Chapter 10

1. Matthew D. Lieberman et al., "Putting Feelings into Words: Affect Labeling Disrupts Amygdala Activity in Response to Affective Stimuli," *Psychological Science* 18, no. 5 (2007): 421-28, doi:10.1111/j.1467-9280.2007.01916.x.

2. Douglas E. Noll, *De-Escalate: How to Calm an Angry Person in 90 Seconds or Less* (Hillsboro, Oregon: Atria Books, 2017).

Chapter 11

1. Jack Balswick and Judith Balswick, *The Family: A Christian Perspective on the Contemporary Home* (Grand Rapids, MI: Baker Publishing, 2014).

2. Ken Sande and Tom Raabe, *Peacemaking for Families* (Carol Stream, IL: Tyndale House, 2002).

3. US Department of State:" Active Listening," accessed on August 26, 2018, from https://www.state.gov/m/a/os/65759.htm.

Chapter 13

1. Johns Hopkins Medicine, "Forgiveness: Your Health Depends on It," accessed April 14, 2020, https://www.hopkinsmedicine.org/health/ wellness-and-prevention/forgiveness-your-health-depends-on-it.
2. Ibid.
3. Martina A. Waltman et al., "The Effects of a Forgiveness Intervention on Patients with Coronary Artery Disease," *Psychology & Health* 24, no. 1 (February 18, 2009): 11-27. doi:10.1080/08870440801975127.
4. Megan F. Bettencourt, "The Science of Forgiveness: 'When You Don't Forgive You Release All the Chemicals of the Stress Response,'" *salon. com*, August 24, 2015, https://www.salon.com/2015/08/24/the_science_of_ forgiveness_when_you_dont_forgive_you_release_all_the_chemicals_of_ the_stress_response/.
5. *Merriam-Webster OnLine*, s.v. "forgive," accessed September 25, 2018, https://www.merriam-webster.com/dictionary/forgive.
6. Amy R. Sisk, "Rwandan Genocide Survivor Shares Story of Forgiveness," *The Bismarck Tribune*, April 4, 2016, https://bismarcktribune.com/ news/state-and-regional/rwandan-genocide-survivor-shares-story-of- forgiveness/article_d8e4f730-2f03-5308-82bb-e7f495734104.html.
7. "Rwandan Genocide Survivor Shares His Story of Forgiveness at One Young World 2017," accessed October 13, 2017, https://www.youtube.com/ watch?v=MrjQ8qK_DzI.
8. Jack Balswick and Judith Balswick, *The Family: A Christian Perspective on the Contemporary Home* (Grand Rapids, MI: Baker Publishing, 2014).
9. Ibid.

Chapter 14

1. American Psychological Association, "Building Your Resilience," accessed September 24, 2018, http://www.apa.org/helpcenter/road-resilience. aspx.
2. Michael M. Criss et al., "Interdisciplinary and Innovative Approaches to Strengthening Family and Individual Resilience: An Introduction to the Special Issue," *Family Relations* 64, no. 1 (2015): 1-4, doi:10.1111/ fare.12109.
3. *Merriam-Webster OnLine*, s.v. "resilience," accessed September 24, 2018, https://www.merriam-webster.com/dictionary/resilience.

4. Froma Walsh, "Applying a Family Resilience Framework in Training, Practice, and Research: Mastering the Art of the Possible," *Family Process* 55, no. 4 (2016): 616-32, doi:10.111/famp.12260.
5. Walsh, "Applying a Family Resilience," 616-32.
6. Jack Balswick and Judith Balswick, *The Family: A Christian Perspective on the Contemporary Home* (Grand Rapids, MI: Baker Publishing, 2014).
7. Ibid.
8. APA, "Building Your Resilience."
9. Dorothy S. Becvar, *Handbook of Family Resilience* (New York, NY: Springer Science & Media, 2012).
10. Ibid.

Chapter 15

1. "Money Ruining Marriages in America: A Ramsey Solutions Study," accessed February 7, 2018, https://www.daveramsey.com/pr/money-ruining-marriages-in-america.

About the Authors

Angela Mitakidis

Angela teaches graduate courses in mediation, family conflict dynamics, and gender and culture conflict management at the Southern Methodist University (SMU) Master's Program in Dispute Resolution and Conflict Management. She is also an adjunct lecturer for Abilene Christian University's conflict resolution program.

Prior to her work in Texas, Angela worked within the legal and dispute resolution fields in Singapore, where she resided for a number of years. In her native South Africa, she was an attorney. She has over 25 years' management experience in the legal and dispute resolution fields internationally.

Angela has also worked with high schools, locally and internationally, to train peer mediators and implement peer mediation programs. Together with her husband, Angela is also a pre-marital counseling facilitator and earned her Master of Science in Counseling at SMU in 2021.

Angela has a passion to impart critical life skills to others in order to equip them to navigate life more effectively in a world often filled with conflict and pressure. From personal experience, she believes these skills can be learned, practiced and applied successfully.

Angela has been married to the love of her life, Michael, for 30 years. They have two darling children, Keziah and Matthew, and the family resides in the Dallas-Fort Worth metroplex.

Shannon R. Brown

Shannon earned her Bachelor of Science in Psychology from the University of Washington. She worked at an inpatient facility before moving into Personnel Psychology for city government. Following the birth of her first child, Shannon left the traditional workforce but continued her passion of helping others through church ministry, as a natural childbirth instructor, doula and childcare provider.

Shannon loves hiking, music, reading, blogging (shannonrbrown. com/the-blog) and spending time with her family—particularly in a mountainous locale. Being the child of a Coast Guardsman, Shannon lived in several different states, but claims Alaska as her home. Married to her college sweetheart, Aaron, a pilot, shortly following graduation and are the parents of Sierra, her husband Jayson, and Tanner. They currently live in the Dallas-Fort Worth metroplex.